Jan. 2014

D0662071

the Teachable MINUTE

Teachable minutes are treasures that last a lifetime—for both parent and child. Dr. Connie Hebert shows new parents the magic and sparkle of teaching in everyday places with the same creative zeal that makes her many books for school teachers wildly popular. She shows you how to pay attention, share, teach, and care. It's all here—teachable minutes that you never thought of everywhere you go.

Read this book and discover teachable minutes in a daily routine chock-full of fun and BE your child's first and best teacher in 77 places you may never have thought of!

I've watched Connie help teachers catch falling readers and writers for years showing them the way to improve student confidence and performance. Now she brings that same inspiration to parents as she encourages parents, especially new parents, to pick up her personal mantra: "Keep doing great things for kids and literacy!"

—**Dr. Richard Gentry**, consultant, speaker
and author of *Raising Confident Readers*

"Parents are a child's first teacher." …such an awesome responsibility. With love it happens naturally. But even in those situations we can become more thoughtful in our efforts. Dr. Connie Hebert has worked with children for over 30 years, offering guidance that has sparked a passion for learning. Her work in schools has inspired shifts in the way teachers interact with children. Now she turns her attention to support that helps parents become more effective teachers in tender and relaxed ways. Stimulating a love of learning in children engages their thinking and reminds all of us that the human spirit is not designed to sit immobile in desks and bubble in tests. We all need to be out in the world, participating in an exploration of the wonders of life. I encourage you to allow Dr. Hebert to share with you a multitude of ways to foster a love for learning in your children…minute by minute.

—**Richard C. Owen**, President and Publisher, Richard C. Owen Publishers, Inc.

"There is nothing more important than the active role that adults must take in effectively teaching our children. It is critical that responsible adults internalize the many secrets to success in *The Teachable Minute* and use them in their daily interactions with our most precious resource—our kids. Dr. Hebert covers all the bases in maximizing our teachable experiences with young people by using the SHOW-ASK-TEACH rubric, which cultivates curiosity, creativity, and the desire to learn more in our children."

—**Mike Boehm**, Senior Business Development Executive for K-12 Educational Technology Platform & a Parent

The Teachable Minute is a perfect book for me, and for this moment in time. With three young children to manage, including one with special needs, my attention span hovers somewhere between a Tweet and a Facebook post. More than an education manual, better than a parenting book, it's a guide to mixing magic into the daily business of raising kids. Teach them well. This book will help you do it.

—**Vicki Vila**, Writer & Mom

This is the perfect gift for any parent, as Dr. Connie conveniently organizes quick, practical teaching tips in 77 different locations — from grocery stores to the bath tub. Sick of the crying and complaining that accompanies your child's homework most nights? This book is the perfect antidote. *The Teachable Minute* provides parents with informative and authentic learning opportunities. Buy this book, and you'll see how teaching your child can be fun...

—**Dr. Danny Brassell**, America's Leading Reading Ambassador, Founder of The Lazy Readers' Book Club, & a Dad

In today's world of "full-speed ahead" living, Dr. Hebert's book is a "must have" for every parent, caregiver and educator. She combines her many years of experience as an educator and an exceptional mother, to show you how to teach your child something no matter where you are or what you're doing. As an experienced teacher and a mother of two, I highly recommend this book as a resource for both parents and educators for becoming an expert at catching the "teachable minute" so that you can learn how to show, ask, and teach kids something quickly and easily. The secret is out! Don't waste a single minute because that's all it takes to connect with a child and engage them in the world around us!

—**Rebecca Conroy**, Parent, Reading Specialist, & Teacher

Don't reinvent the wheel; use Dr. Hebert's practical pearls for parenting. This book will empower your ability to raise happy kids who appreciate the lives they are blessed with.

—**Dr. Ed Park**, Father & Telomerase and Rejuvenation expert from Recharge Biomedical

the Teachable
MINUTE

The Secret to Raising
Smart & Appreciative Kids

DR. CONNIE HEBERT

NEW YORK

the Teachable MINUTE
The Secret to Raising Smart & Appreciative Kids

ISBN 978-1-61448-469-1 paperback
ISBN 978-1-61448-470-7 eBook
ISBN 978-1-61448-471-4 Audio Book
Library of Congress Control Number: 2012953596

Morgan James Publishing
The Entrepreneurial Publisher
5 Penn Plaza, 23rd Floor
New York City, New York 10001
(212) 655-5470 office • (516) 908-4496 fax
www.MorganJamesPublishing.com

Cover Design by:
Rachel Lopez
www.r2cdesign.com

Interior Design by:
Bonnie Bushman
bonnie@caboodlegraphics.com

In an effort to support local communities, raise awareness and funds, Morgan James Publishing donates a percentage of all book sales for the life of each book to Habitat for Humanity Peninsula and Greater Williamsburg.

Get involved today, visit
www.MorganJamesBuilds.com.

Dedicated to Dorothy,

who caught the teachable minute with
three characters,

on a yellow brick road,

and learned that she always had the
power within,

to go home . . .

TABLE OF CONTENTS

ACKNOWLEDGEMENTS

It is my sincerest hope that this book will enlighten, motivate, and excite parents about catching precious, fleeting 'teachable minutes' with their children every single day…

Heartfelt thanks to my loving parents, Artemis & Michael Romell, for being my first and most important teachers. I am so happy you are both here to see this book completed! Thank you for everything.

To my many phenomenal teachers, beautiful students, caring family members, and supportive friends: Thank you for making time to catch many 'teachable minutes' with me, as I have grown.

Words cannot express my love and appreciation to my husband, David, for his constant support and encouragement along the journey. To our three incredible kids: Thank you, kids, for paying close attention to Dad and me while we caught so many 'teachable minutes' with each one of you. I have truly loved being Tiffany, Gabriel, and Daniel's mother and first teacher. It worked! You are all smart, caring, and appreciative young adults. I have no doubt you will do the same for your kids.

I am so grateful to Scott Frishman, Rick Frishman, David Hancock, and all the good people at Morgan James Publishing for believing in the concept of The Teachable Minute. You are amazing, caring, inspiring men. You changed my direction and lightened my path.

Special thanks to Lorraine for her support and talents, once again.

This book was built with love and friendship from my dearest friends, Grace & Di…and my wise teacher, 'Stargazer.'

Thank you, God, for good health, vision, wisdom . . . and perseverance.

WHAT IS
the Teachable MINUTE?

THE TEACHABLE MINUTE is a golden opportunity to teach kids something, anywhere, FAST. It can be caught at any time, in common places, where we all live and go. It appears in a car, at the mall, around the kitchen table, at the post office, in the yard, on a plane, in an elevator, at the beach, on the subway, in a rocking chair, at the park, in the bathtub, and anywhere else you can think of.

ALL kids are naturally curious.

ALL kids want attention.

When we make time to SHOW, ASK, or TEACH kids something, we help kids in two very important ways:

- We help them grow smarter. Consequently, they will know more and want to know more.
- We cultivate appreciation because we give them time and undivided attention. Consequently, they will grow appreciative and grateful for our efforts.

You may have heard the phrase "the teachable moment." I brought the concept to a new level because I believe kids deserve longer than a moment of our time. All children, no matter how old, are capable of being taught, and they are surely worth at least a minute of our time in a variety of settings. Hence, the teachable minute was born!

Here are 3 important questions to consider as you search for teachable minutes with kids:

1. *What do I want my kids to know about this place or thing?*
2. *Where is the best place to catch the teachable minute today, for this child?*
3. *How do I want my kids to remember time spent with me?*

During the last few years, I've spoken with hundreds of parents and teachers to get a better idea of how kids connect with them on a daily basis. Many of them shared their growing concern about the constant use of cell phones and other devices, especially when kids are around. I share this concern. Everywhere we go, we can find kids who are watching adults who are engaging with devices at all hours of the day and night—using cell phones, responding to text messages, surfing the web, responding to email, and watching a lot of television.

This concern raised an important question for me:

How can we strike a BALANCE between engaging with devices and interacting with kids?

As I considered the answer, I drew from many years as a mother of three children, experienced educator, and national literacy consultant. I've caught thousands, if not millions, of teachable minutes with kids! What I know for sure is that when we make a conscious effort to capture the teachable minute as often as possible and in a variety of settings, we help kids grow smart and appreciative.

Here is the answer to my question:

We must limit the use of devices when kids are with us and make time to SHOW, ASK, and TEACH them something, wherever we are. Kids will learn that technology is a good thing but it is not the most important thing. THEY are!

Recently, I had lunch in a local restaurant. I noticed a young boy who was seated across from his mother. He was coloring a picture while asking questions and telling her all kinds of neat things. She did not respond or even look up at him once; she was totally engaged with her cell phone. For me, the saddest part came when the boy began moving his crayon very quickly across the paper. He looked up at his Mom and shouted, "Look, Mom, I'm growing muscles!" I felt badly for both of them because the teachable minute came…and went.

It is my sincerest hope that as you catch the teachable minute with your kids, you will discover the following:

- *M*ore spontaneous fun
- *I*ncreased self-confidence in the role of 'parent as teacher'
- *N*umerous opportunities to interact with kids in memorable ways
- *U*npredictable benefits that will lead to lifelong learning
- *T*ime with kids so they feel important, valued, and special
- *E*ndless waves of satisfaction that come when we make a difference in the life of a child

How This Book Works

My goal is to help you become an expert at catching **THE TEACHABLE MINUTE** so that you can interact with kids of all ages, anytime and anywhere. The simple format of the book makes it quick and easy to learn. Once you try out some of these ideas, you may want to make up some of your own. Before you know it, you'll be catching the teachable minute without even knowing that you are!

Here's how it works:

- The book is divided into 5 main categories:
  - ◊ **Our Town**
  - ◊ **Our Home**
  - ◊ **Public Places**
  - ◊ **Recreation Spots**
  - ◊ **Transportation**
- Under each category, you will find common places that we are all familiar with. There are **77 places** to choose from.
- Pick a place where you happen to be, are planning to go, or just simply want to explore with kids.
- Read my suggestions for what to **SHOW**, **ASK**, and **TEACH** your kids. *Note: These are only suggestions to help*

you get started. Add to them as you go along. Be creative and have fun!

- Catch **THE TEACHABLE MINUTE** as often as possible in as many places as possible and see what happens. It's that simple!

REMEMBER: S * A * T
Show
Ask
Teach

I have included comments and touching stories from many people who shared their teachable minute with me. My hope is that will help you connect with others, just like you, who want to catch the teachable minute with kids, before it's too late.

Be sure to check out my tips *Especially for Moms* and *Especially for Dads*. Why did I create these, you might ask? Well, Moms and Dads are uniquely different and special in their own wonderful ways! They have specific interests, individual communication styles, and differences in how they engage with kids. You will find tips for both throughout the book. You will also see a few tips that are *Especially for Grandparents*. Have fun catching the teachable minute together!

If you use many of the suggestions in the book as often as possible, I guarantee that you will learn how to:

- *R*ecognize a teachable minute when it comes along
- *E*mbrace opportunities to share what you know
- *A*ctively engage with kids so they feel important and special

- *C*atch a bunch of good questions to help kids 'think'
- *H*elp kids use their natural curiosity and imagination

If we are going to successfully launch children into a technologically complex, fast-paced, literate world, we must keep our eye firmly ON THE CHILD. We want all kids to be smart and appreciative adults as they contribute to society in their own unique ways. We must catch the teachable minute no matter where we are. Once it's gone, it's gone.

THE TEACHABLE MINUTE is right around the corner, waiting to be caught. Turn the page and follow me . . .

To bring Dr. Connie to your conference, event, or school district, please visit: www.conniehebert.com

For details on how to receive free downloadable materials, please visit: www.theteachableminute.com

AROUND TOWN

When we catch the teachable minute near and around the place where kids live, they grow up feeling like they 'own' their childhood experiences.

INSTILL BELONGING...

For more information on how to INSTILL BELONGING with your kids visit:
theteachableminute.com/instill

ATM MACHINE

◇◇◇◇◇◇◇◇◇◇◇◇◇◇◇◇◇◇◇◇◇◇◇◇◇◇◇◇◇◇◇◇

"My daughter wanted to go back to the amusement park and I told her we didn't have any money to do that again so soon. She looked up at me and replied, "Well Dad, just go to the ATM. There's lots of money in it!"

—Michael, Miami Beach, FL

YOUNGER KIDS

SHOW them things on the machine like the number key pad. Have them point to each key while saying each number aloud. Then have them point and say again, going backwards. Point to numbers on the screen and have them 'point and say' them with you. Count money together!

ASK questions such as, "How do you think the money gets into the ATM machine? How many dollar bills have to come out of the machine for us to get five dollars?" "Can you show me the number 2 on the keypad?" "Can you show me where the money comes out?"

TEACH them how to punch in deposit or withdrawal amounts as you press each key and count out loud together (example: to deposit $100.00, press the keypad while saying aloud, "ONE, ZERO, ZERO, DECIMAL POINT, ZERO ZERO").

OLDER KIDS

SHOW them things like how to fill out a deposit/withdrawal slip or envelope or how to count cash as it comes out of the machine. Encourage them to look for details on a dollar bill. What do they all have in common? What's different?

ASK questions such as, "Why do you think people have to sign their name on the back of checks when they deposit them? What's the difference between a deposit and a withdrawal?" "What do you think ATM stands for and why did someone call it that?"

TEACH them things like how to deposit a check and get cash back or how to check the balance in the account. Help them fill out a withdrawal or deposit form and show them the steps that are necessary to make that happen. Kids see adults at ATM machines all the time. It can be an interesting teacher!

BANK

◇◇◇◇◇◇◇◇◇◇◇

Especially for Dads: *Kids love when you show them HOW to roll coins. What can they learn from doing this?*
Especially for Moms: *The car is a great place to talk to kids about WHY people save money. Do they know what the purpose of a piggy bank is? Can they think of things they would like to save up for?*

YOUNGER KIDS

SHOW them how to sort money. Have them sort different types of coins and paper money by placing them in separate piles and then counting them with you. Kids like to sort things. Use paper plates to have them sort pennies, dimes, and quarters.

ASK questions such as, "What does the word, bank, begin with?" "Can you think of another word that starts like bank?" "What words rhyme with bank?" "How many letters are in bank?" "What's the last letter in bank?"

TEACH them the names of things in a bank, and what they mean, in order to build vocabulary and enlarge understandings of concepts such as bank teller, drive-up window, deposit slip, envelope, ATM, vault, computer monitor, manager, etc.

OLDER KIDS

SHOW them how to endorse the back of a check and how to write out the amount in 'words' (example: $125.70 = One hundred twenty-five dollars & seventy cents.) Give them lots of practice with this. Kids need to define their own signature for signing important documents. What will it look like?

ASK questions such as, "What does a bank teller do?" "How do you think money gets from a company to the bank every day?" "What does an armored car look like?" "Why do people who drive armored cars have to be responsible and trustworthy?"

TEACH things like how to read a bank statement, defining what credit, debit, deposit, and balance mean. Too many teens do not know what these things are or how to manage their money. Let's fix that!

BUS STOP

◇◇◇◇◇◇◇◇◇◇◇◇◇◇◇◇◇◇◇◇◇

I've been at the bus stop for all of three minutes and I've counted eight people on their cell phones. That is amazing to me.

—K. Wald, Twitter Mom

YOUNGER KIDS

SHOW things that represent the season while you wait at the bus stop such as colored leaves on trees, jackets or sweaters on kids, and closed car windows the fall. No seasons? Point out different shapes around you such as rectangular windows, square houses, round manholes, oval street lights, and a square lunch box.

ASK them things like, "What would you do if something happens and I was late when the bus came to our stop at the end of the day?" "What is a nice thing to say to the bus driver when you get on and off the bus?" "Why do some kids cry on the bus?"

TEACH them about being kind and friendly to other kids on the bus. Pretend that you are a kid on the bus and you're sitting next to each other. Role-play how to start a conversation...and how to keep it going!

OLDER KIDS

SHOW them different street markings at the bus stop so they become familiar with their meaning such as a crosswalk, breakdown lanes, solid divider lines versus broken divider lines, a yield sign, a yellow street light, a blinking red light, etc.

ASK questions that require more than a one-word answer such as, "Why do you think someone would want to drive a bus?" "Why do you think most school buses don't have seatbelts for kids to wear?"

TEACH them about what to do if a stranger approaches them on the way to the bus stop. You might role-play different scenarios or tell them stories about different things that have happened to kids. Too many people think that older kids already know these things, but many of them forget all the wisdom we taught them when they were toddlers. Repetition is good… and necessary!

CAR WASH

Especially for Dads: *Do they know how the car is pulled through the car wash? Show them!*

Especially for Moms: *This is a great time to 'sing in the rain'... Sing songs as you go through the car wash. Do they know which song is your favorite song, Mom?*

YOUNGER KIDS

SHOW them all the different machines that are designed specifically to wash a car. Point out different things as you go through the car wash so they learn new words such as, bubbles, brushes, sprayers, blow dryers, and machines.

ASK them questions like, "How could we wash our car if there weren't any car washes?" "What tools would we need?" "Why do we wash our car?" "What happens if we don't wash our car?"

TEACH the names of different parts of the car that are being washed such as roof, hood, windshield, windows, tires, side-view mirrors, trunk, etc. Even if they can't talk yet, they are listening. Keep pointing at things. They will tell you what they are if you keep it up.

OLDER KIDS

SHOW them the track where the wheels will fit before you fully enter the carwash. The attendant will wait a minute while you explain how the left wheels run in a track as the car is pushed by a mechanical device behind the left back tire.

ASK them things like "How do you think these machines know WHEN to spray, turn, move, scrub, and dry?" "Why do you think more people like the car wash better than washing it themselves?" "Who are the people who invent car wash machines?" "Do you think they are charging a fair price for a car wash or not? What makes you think so?"

TEACH them chores such as how to vacuum the mats, wash the car windows, check the oil, fill the tires with air, and clean the dashboard. Then let them do it the best way that they can and they will want to do it again...hopefully!

COFFEE SHOP

My Nana use to take me to a coffee shop for a bagel with cream cheese and gummy bears. I remember how she taught me lots of things while we were there like how to count my gummy bears and how to spread cream cheese on my bagel. But, what I loved most was when she took me across the street to see "Mr. Clockie." This clock was taller than tall and she taught me all about its 'face.' I learned the value of THE TEACHABLE MINUTE with my Grandmother.

—Joe, Roslindale, MA

YOUNGER KIDS

SHOW them the different categories of foods and drinks on the sign or menu. For example, muffins, bagels, donuts, drinks, condiments, etc. If there are signs, point out letters, sounds, and words. Signs are great teachers!

ASK them things like, "How do you think a baker makes a bagel?" "Why do you think they call it a coffee shop?" "What do you think they should have in the coffee shop for kids to look at?"

TEACH them how to pay for what they want to eat and drink at the coffee shop…and count the change together. You may want to let them pretend that they are selling you a bagel or a muffin. What do they need to know? Younger kids love to take food orders!

OLDER KIDS

SHOW them the set-up of the furniture in the coffee shop. Discuss how it is different from a restaurant and why. What else do they notice about on the walls, bulletin boards, windows, and doors?

ASK them questions such as, "What do you think they have to do to get ready to open the shop every morning?" or "Why would someone want to own a coffee shop instead of a store or a restaurant?"

TEACH them how to estimate the cost of coffee shop items so they know about how much something will cost when they go up to the counter to order. For example, if a bagel is $3.65 and orange juice is $1.75, they would round the bagel price up to $4.00 and the orange juice up to $2.00. Better have around $6.00 that day!

FAST FOOD DRIVE-UP

Especially for Dads: *Kids are naturally curious about the way the server can hear the driver. Can you explain that?*
Especially for Moms: *This is a great time to do some 'singing in the rain'...teach a new song!*

YOUNGER KIDS

SHOW them the drive-thru lane and talk about how it is different from other parts of the parking lot. Point out the speaker, menu board, and cashier. Kids are watching and taking things in as we go through a drive-thru.

ASK them things like, "What is your favorite sandwich, your favorite drink, and your favorite kids' meal?" Tell them what your favorite sandwich, drive, and dessert is. Ask them why adults can't get kids' meals? You may be surprised at what they tell you!

TEACH them how to count to 100 (forwards and backwards) while you are waiting for your food. Then try counting by 2's, 5's, and 10's. Do this repeatedly when you are in drive-up lines. What else have you got to do?!

OLDER KIDS

SHOW them the giant menu as you drive by it and talk about why value meals, kids' meals, and/or combination meals are offered.

ASK questions such as, "Why do you think drive-up windows were invented?" "What would happen if they closed all the drive-up windows and people had to go inside?" "How is a fast food place different from a restaurant?"

TEACH kids about various objects in the car and their functions while waiting in the drive-up line for your order, for example, turn signals, side-view mirrors, cruise control, back window defroster, etc. Ask them about what type of car they would like to have, and why.

GAS STATION

My kids always fight in the car while I am putting gas in the car. It never fails! They either find something to argue about, grab from one another, or disagree about something. I guess they are learning how to be in a confined space with no adult in that space! One day I got in the car and heard the disagreement that was still going on between my daughter and son. He was screaming, "NO! It's MY diarrhea!" She was trying to convince him that diarrhea "doesn't belong to you!!!!" He could not be convinced. We left the gas station with him still screaming, "No! It's MY diarrhea!"

—A New Mom, Watch Hill, RI

YOUNGER KIDS

SHOW them the gas pump and how it works. Kids love to see what is going on when we fill up.

ASK questions like, "How do you think I know when the car needs gas?" "What does 'F' stand for and what does 'E' stand for?" "Can you think of another word that starts like the word, full?" "Do 'empty' and 'elephant' start with the sound?" "What other word starts like that?"

TEACH them how to look at the gas price on the pump and say it correctly: "Three dollars and eighty-five cents." Point to the numbers as you say them aloud.

OLDER KIDS

SHOW them how to determine which side of a car the gas pump is on by letting them look at the speedometer to find the little picture of a gas pump. It will show whether the gas goes on the right or the left!

ASK questions such as, "If the tank shows there is a quarter of a tank left, how much gas did we use?" "If the price of gas is $3.00, then how much will it cost to fill up a 12-gallon tank?" "If we run out of gas, what should we do?"

TEACH them how to round up the price of a gallon of gas so they can learn to estimate how much money they would need to fill the tank. For example, if the price is $3.98, they will round that up to $4.00. If they put 10 gallons of gas in the tank, approximately how much money do they need?

GROCERY STORE

Especially for Dads: *Point out cool stuff in the store such as the lobster tank, the deli slicer machines, magazine racks, fruit scale, and food conveyor belt. Cool!*

Especially for Moms: *Take a tour of the flower section, pointing out different types of flowers and plants. Beautiful!*

YOUNGER KIDS

SHOW them how items are arranged in categories: cereals, dairy products, fruits, vegetables, meats, baking goods, paper products, frozen foods, etc.

ASK them things like, "What is your favorite kind of cookie?" "Where does milk come from?" "Where do eggs come from?" "How many apples do we need? Let's count them as we put them in the bag."

TEACH them how to count eggs in an egg carton and how to check for cracked eggs. Tell them some of the reasons why eggs break. See if they can come up with some reasons, too.

OLDER KIDS

SHOW them how cereal is arranged. Are they alphabetically placed on shelves? Are they arranged by the company that makes them? Are they arranged by which ones kids like the most?

ASK questions such as, "How do we know where to find things in the store?" "What category would you look for if you wanted to find trash bags or ice cream or shampoo?" "How do we know which deli meats are on sales?" "What's a coupon for?"

TEACH them how a fruit and vegetable scale works. Help them figure out how many apples it takes for a total of 2 pounds and how much that will cost. Let them weigh items like a melon, a potato, a grapefruit, an onion, and a tomato. Then ask, "What did you discover?"

HARDWARE STORE

I took my son to a hardware store to teach him about tools. I wanted him to know what a wrench is for, what a screwdriver can do, and what the proper tool is for cutting wire. His Mom uses a butter knife, scissors, or whatever happens to be lying around to fix things. So I figured I'd better teach him that there's a proper tool for every job!

—Jack, Denver, CO

YOUNGER KIDS

SHOW them different items around the store by holding them up and naming them. (Example: shovel, hammer, rake, bird feeder, paintbrush, flashlight, anything!)

ASK them things like, "Why do you think we need a hose for our yard?" "What is the sound that a hammer makes?" "How many hammers do you see hanging up?"

TEACH them how to turn a flashlight on and off. What other devices have an ON/OFF button? How fun is this?!

OLDER KIDS

SHOW them different types of nails and screws and point out why they are shaped differently.

ASK questions that make them think about similarities and differences such as "How are birdfeeders the same and different?" "How are paintbrushes the same and different?" "How are light bulbs the same and different?" Let them look closely at these objects while you point out certain features.

TEACH them how to compare prices for similar tools. For example, point out the hammer that is the most expensive and the one that is least expensive. What makes one more expensive than the other? What features make them different?

ICE CREAM SHOP

<><><><><><><><><><><><><><><><><><><><><><><><><><><>

Especially for Dads: *Share a book or You Tube video about how ice cream is made in today's world. Kids love to see how machines work. Then go get ice cream together!*

Especially for Moms: *Have a taste testing event in your kitchen, blindfolded. Fun! Let kids test 3 different kinds of ice creams and vote for their favorite one. Which one is the winner?*

YOUNGER KIDS

SHOW them what a plain cone looks like and what a sugar cone looks like. Plain, Sugar, Plain, Sugar!

ASK questions about colors: "What color is vanilla (chocolate, strawberry, and pistachio) ice cream?" Then stretch their thinking by asking "What color is snow (dirt, an apple, a banana, grass)?"

TEACH them how to scoop some of their ice cream with a spoon. What does 'scooping' something mean?" "What do we use to 'scoop' sand at the beach or in the sandbox?" Let's scoop!

OLDER KIDS

SHOW them how ice cream flavors are listed. Then see if they could make up a new flavor. What would it taste like and look like?

ASK questions like "Why does ice cream melt?" "What did they do before they had freezers to freeze things?" "How are plain cones and sugar cones different?" "If you could invent a new ice cream flavor, what would it be called?"

TEACH them how to alphabetize ice cream flavors. Make a list of all the ice cream flavors the shop has and put them in A-B-C order together. Another idea would be to play a game where they have to guess what kind of ice cream you are thinking of by asking you questions that could be answered ONLY with a 'yes' or a 'no.'

LAUNDROMAT

"My daughter use to sit on a chair at the laundromat as she watched the clothes go round and round in the dryer. She always had a scowl on her face as she sucked on her index finger and rocked back and forth. I just know she was thinking why, oh why, is my precious 'blankie' in that thing and why can't I have it right NOW...ah, kids and blankets share loving moments."

—Tamika, Houston, TX

Younger Kids

SHOW them how to put the money in the washers and dryers, counting each coin that is pushed in. Then show them where the START button or dial is. Kids love to push buttons and turn dials!

ASK questions such as, "Why do we have to put clothes in the dryer?" "Why do the clothes feel warm when they come out of the dryer?" "Why do we wash our clothes?"

TEACH them how to fold clothes. Face towels and wash cloths are easy to fold in half and then in half again. This is the way we fold the clothes!

OLDER KIDS

SHOW them how to set the washer and dryer cycles to the right settings.

ASK them questions that make them think about different parts related to a washer and dryer. Examples: "What is the lint collector for and why do we have to empty it?" "Why does a washing machine spin?" "Where does the laundry detergent go?"

TEACH them how to sort clothes into different piles and how to choose the right machine for the right pile of clothes. How much soap does each load need and does it go? How much money does each machine need and how does a change machine work? There's a lot to learn here!

LIBRARY

◇◇◇◇◇◇◇◇◇◇◇◇◇◇◇◇◇

Especially for Dads: *Consider taking kids to the children's section of the library and help them pick out books they think they would like to own, based on their interests. Take pictures of the front covers with your cell phone or camera so that you create a 'wish list' of books for birthday or holiday gifts.*

Especially for Moms: *Why not find a quiet corner in the library (even the floor will do) and read a classic picture book together? Memories of reading in the library together will last a long time, for both of you!*

YOUNGER KIDS

SHOW kids the way to stack all the books that are going home with you. Start from the bottom, counting aloud as you stack and count together.

ASK questions such as, "Where do we go to check out our books?" "How many books are we taking home?" "What letter does LIBRARY start with?" "Can you think of other words that start like LIBRARY?"

TEACH them how to find a favorite book on the library shelf. What letters are in the title of the book? How many pages are in the book? Where is the front and the back of the book?

OLDER KIDS

SHOW them how to use the library computer to find books on a subject they are interested in. They may need help with comparing several books on the same subject. How are they alike and different?

ASK questions about the library. For example, "How are books organized on the shelves?" "Where would we find books about tornadoes, mammals, and China?" "What happens if you don't return a book to the library on time?" "What happens if you lose a book that you checked out?" "What are the differences between a library and an online bookstore?"

TEACH them about book jackets. What's the purpose of a book jacket? What information is located on inside flaps of a book jacket? Point out the features on the back cover. Can they design their own book jacket on a rainy day?

NEIGHBORHOOD

◇◇◇◇◇◇◇◇◇◇◇◇◇◇◇◇◇◇◇◇◇◇◇◇◇◇◇◇◇◇◇◇◇◇◇◇◇◇

One fall morning while my kids and I were walking down the sidewalk on our way to PS82 (upper west side), my 5 year old stopped suddenly and said, "Hey, Mom. How does a street sweeper work?" I knew, then and there, that he would probably be an engineer. He never liked fictitious stories or novels. He only wanted to read books about how things work! That made me think about how important it is for us to 'know' our kids and to tap into their interests with books that will motivate and engage them. He's 26 now…and yes, an engineer.

—Marilyn, NYC

YOUNGER KIDS

SHOW them how to 'point and say' what things are as you take a walk around the neighborhood. Examples for this would be a mailbox, fire hydrant, driveway, store, street sign, stop sign, traffic light, sidewalk, yard, playground, school, church, flag, tree, car, bus, bicycle, basketball hoop, airplane, etc. POINT and SAY, POINT and SAY, POINT and SAY!

ASK questions that lead to predictions such as, "Why do you think the squirrel buries nuts?" "How does a bird make a nest up in a tree?" "How does the mail get into the mailbox?"

TEACH them how to STOP, LOOK BOTH WAYS, GO, LOOK AGAIN, as you cross streets in the neighborhood. Have them say the words with you: "STOP"… "LOOK BOTH WAYS"… "GO"… "LOOK AGAIN"

OLDER KIDS

SHOW them different kinds of cars or stores or houses there are in your neighborhood. Name them together.

ASK them about things that lead them to evaluate why people like what they like. For example, "Why do you think some people like houses that don't have stairs in them?" "Why do some people like to live up high in apartments and other people like houses?" "Why do you some people prefer to take a bus to work?" "Why do some people prefer the city to the country?"

TEACH them street names in the neighborhood. This can be done while driving through the neighborhood or by looking at a map together. What do they notice? How would they get from one place to another? What's the fastest route from our house to the bank? Mapping skills are important, even with the invention of the GPS!

PLAYGROUND

<><><><><><><><><><><><><><><><><><><>

Especially for Grandparents: Share stories what their mother or father liked, and didn't like, when they were little. Kids love to learn about when their parents were like as kids. Grandparents can serve as a bridge that connects kids with their parents in wonderful ways. True!

YOUNGER KIDS

SHOW them how to pull back and forth, with their legs and arms, in order to make a swing go higher.

ASK questions that help them solve problems such as, "What can you do to go faster on the slide?" "Where should you put your thumbs when you climb a ladder so you won't fall?" "What can you do with your arms so you keep your balance on a balance beam or a bridge walk?"

TEACH them how to LOOK UP and to WATCH THEIR STEP when they are climbing. That's good advice on the playground and in life!

OLDER KIDS

SHOW them different types of playgrounds either in a book or on the internet. Point out likes and differences.

ASK questions that lead them to thinking about others as they play at a playground such as, "What should you do if a kid is sitting at the top of the slide and won't go down?" "What should you do if you want to walk in front (or in back) of a kid who is swinging on a swing?" "What would you say to kids who won't let you have a turn?" "How could you help a kid who is hurt at the playground?"

TEACH them about the value of a playground for staying healthy, in shape, and in tune with what their bodies need. Talk about why we have playgrounds in the world? Ask if they have any ideas for new playground equipment. Can they draw what they envision? Encourage imagination.

POST OFFICE

◇◇◇◇◇◇◇◇◇◇◇◇◇◇◇◇◇◇◇◇◇◇◇◇◇◇◇◇◇◇◇◇

The Post Office Book: Mail and How It Moves by Gail Gibbons. I read this book to my kids at breakfast. Then I encouraged them to draw a picture and write a letter to their favorite author. I went online and found publishers for the authors. I got envelopes and wrote the publishers' addresses on each. Then I helped them fold, stuff, and seal their envelopes. Next, we wrote the name of the author under the word: ATTENTION. After putting a stamp on each envelope, we headed for the post office to mail them. We heard back from all 3 authors! The kids were thrilled and they even brought their 'author's letter' to school to share. I am so glad I did this. Not only did my kids learn how to prepare and mail a letter, they learned that authors are 'real' people who care about fan mail!

—Kelly, Houston, TX

YOUNGER KIDS

SHOW them how to open and close the large post office boxes on the sidewalk. Say "open" and "close" each time. Have them say "open" and "close" with you. Then say, "Show me OPEN. Now show me CLOSE." These are important concepts!

ASK questions like, "What does the mail man do?" "Why do we have a mailbox?" "What sound does MAIL start with?" "What other words start like MAIL? Let's name them."

TEACH them how to ask for stamps at the post office counter and how to put a stamp on the top right corner of an envelope.

OLDER KIDS

SHOW them how to find different numbers on post office boxes in the post office. Say, "Show me Box #222." "Show me Box #52." "Show me all the boxes that have a 2 in them." "Show me all the boxes that are multiples of ten: #10, #20, #30, #40, etc."

ASK them questions that help them think about the role of mail and why it is private property. Examples: "Why do you think it's against the law to open someone's mailbox?" "What are the only days in the year when we don't get mail?" "Why do some people have post office boxes at the post office?"

TEACH them how to address an envelope, including the return address. Discuss what information MUST be on the envelope in order for it to be delivered and what happens to it if that information is not there.

SCHOOL

"While we are walkin' to school, I use the time to teach my kids whatever I want to. I feel this makes them better listeners, better writers, and better thinkers. I ask them lots of questions."

—LaTonya-Ocoee, FL

Especially for Dads: *Tell them facts about bullying. What is a bully? What are some ways to handle a bully? Why do some kids not tell their parents they are being bullied?*
Especially for Moms: *Share some personal lessons you learned when you were a kid in school.*

YOUNGER KIDS

SHOW them the main rooms in a school. If you can't take them to a school, show them in a book or online. Have them say the name of the room as you point out library, cafeteria, school office, gym, auditorium, bathroom, and music room.

ASK questions that will help them know the names of various people who can help them in a school. For example, "Who helps us in school when we feel sick?" "Who teaches us how to read and write?" "Who cleans the school?" "Who is in charge of the school?"

TEACH them how to pick out things around the house for 'Show and Tell' time. Even if they don't go to school, you can have 'Show and Tell' at home, once a week. Demonstrate what YOU would 'show and tell' if you had to show something and tell others about it. Modeling works!

OLDER KIDS

SHOW them the neighborhood and main streets around their school. Many kids don't actually know where the school is located in the town. If they had to walk somewhere near the school to get help, where should they go? Show them.

ASK a few open-ended questions that will require more than a one-word answer. For example, instead of saying, "How was your day?" ask, "How was today different from yesterday?" or "What was the best thing that happened in school today, and the worst?"

TEACH them how to make a list of all of the things they need to do for the coming week. This is list of reminders, events, appointments, chores, and responsibilities. You will want to suggest that they list any items they will need to bring to school on any given day. For example, a baseball glove on Tuesday, a newspaper article on Thursday, or canned goods for the food drive on Friday.

AT HOME

We help kids appreciate the home we have made for them by catching the teachable minute in every room.

MODEL APPRECIATION...

For more information on how to
MODEL APPRECIATION with your kids visit:
theteachableminute.com/model

A GOOD CHAIR

◇◇◇◇◇◇◇◇◇◇◇◇◇◇◇◇◇◇◇◇◇◇◇◇◇◇◇◇◇◇◇◇

"My Grandmother used to sit for hours by the window, sewing, reading, or crocheting. Sometimes I thought the chair was doing the rocking! Maybe there is something to be learned while sitting in a 'good chair'… or maybe a 'good chair' is needed for us to learn something. I wonder."
—Sandra, Hamilton, MT

YOUNGER KIDS

SHOW them pictures in a book or on the internet of all the different kinds of chairs. Make a point to show them chairs, wherever you go. Ever notice how kids like to climb on chairs?!

ASK them questions such as, "Is this a high chair or low chair?" "Is this a rocking chair or a kitchen chair?" "Is this a big chair or little chair?" "Is this your chair?" Correct them if they guess wrong. They will get each one if you keep at it long enough.

TEACH them how to push a chair in and pull it out. Have them say the words, "push" and "pull," as they push the chair in and pull the chair out. Do the same in a rocker. Rock the chair while saying, "forward" and "backward." Do the same in a swivel chair. Swivel the chair while saying "right" and "left."

OLDER KIDS

SHOW kids the differences that exist among chairs: some have 'arms,' others have a straight back and 'legs,' some rock, some swivel, some have seat cushions, others are made of wood or metal, some have levers to make them go up and down, and others can fold up. Lots of differences!

ASK questions that help kids with predictions such as, "Why do you think chairs were invented?" "What kind of chairs do you think Grandparents like best? Why?" "When do you think a chair should be thrown away?"

TEACH them how to find a **good** chair, a **good** book, and a **good** light. Share your likes and dislikes and encourage kids to do the same. This will serve them well when making choices for themselves.

BASEMENT

◇◇◇◇◇◇◇◇◇◇◇◇◇◇◇◇◇◇◇◇◇◇◇◇◇◇◇

"Kids are naturally curious about basements. Basements are usually darker than the rest of the house and they don't look the same. One day when my kids were helping me with the laundry down in the basement, my youngest suddenly ran up the basement stairs, opened the door, and then came back down. He exclaimed, "Hey Mom. We are having 6 more weeks of summer!" "Really," I said. "How do you know?" "Because I ran up from our hole, saw my shadow in the hallway, and came back down. My teacher told us that the groundhog does the same thing when it's winter." I smiled…and would you believe, we did have a very hot fall that year?!"

—Susan, Virginia Beach, VA

YOUNGER KIDS

SHOW them how to count the number of stairs as you climb up and down. You can even count backwards as you climb…and by twos.

ASK questions to help them identify objects in the basement such as, "Where is the washing machine/dryer?" Then, for confirmation, point and say, "There it is." "Where is the couch/chair?" "There it is." "Where is the light?" "There it is." "Where is the pipe?" "There it is."

TEACH them the concept of ON and OFF or OPEN and CLOSE using a light switch, washing machine lid, clothes dryer door, water faucet, hatchway door, flashlight, radio, television, closet door, and anything else you can find in the basement that teaches the concept of ON and OFF or OPEN and CLOSE.

OLDER KIDS

SHOW them the appliances and important household items that are in a basement such as the furnace, water heater, fuse box, pipe valves, hatchway door, tools, smoke alarm, fire extinguisher, sporting equipment, holiday decorations, a fire extinguisher, and anything else that will help them know where things can be found in the case of an emergency. Many kids don't know what is in the basement and their natural curiosity can get them into trouble if they don't know what is what!

ASK questions such as "Why do you think it's darker or colder in the basement than in the kitchen?" "Why do so many houses and buildings have basements?" "Why are the windows smaller in a basement than they are in the rest of the house?"

TEACH them how to operate a washer and dryer. Many kids do not know how until they are teenagers! There is much to be learned from these amazing machines.

BATHROOM

◇◇◇◇◇◇◇◇◇◇◇◇◇◇◇◇◇◇◇◇◇◇◇◇◇◇

Did you ever try to teach a child how to fold a big bath towel? At 5 years old, my son wanted to show me that he knew how to do it just by watching me. He tried but could not get it like he wanted it. I sat down on the bathroom rug with him, right then and there, and spread out the towel. Together, we brought up the two bottom corners to meet the top two corners, brought the folded part up to the top part of the towel, and then in half. "Thanks Mama," he said ---and off he went. He never talked about it again. But to this day, I'm convinced that every time he picks up a folded towel, he remembers that teachable minute with me on the bathroom floor.

—Artemis, Longmeadow, MA

YOUNGER KIDS

SHOW them the difference between the cold faucet and the hot faucet. Teach the concept of HOT and COLD. Come up with other words that start like 'hot' and 'cold.'

ASK them questions that help them think about the importance of being clean! For example, "Why do we wash our hands after we go to the bathroom?" "What will happen if we don't brush out teeth every day?" "What does dental floss do?" "How much shampoo do you need in your hand to make your hair clean and shiny?"

TEACH them how to scrub the bathroom tub. They can do it if you teach them how!

OLDER KIDS

SHOW them several different kinds of soap. Let them examine, smell, touch, and use them. Which one do they prefer to use? Let them choose and maybe they will use soap more often!

ASK questions that lead to critical thinking. For instance, "How does the water reach the bathtub faucet?" "What would you do if the toilet overflowed or the sink clogged?" "If we used up one toilet paper roll every two days, how many toilet paper rolls do we need for one week?"

TEACH them how the toilet works! Kids really don't know. It's fascinating to see their faces when we remove the lid and show them what happens when we flush. It's a mystery!

BATHTUB

✧✧✧✧✧✧✧✧✧✧✧✧✧✧✧✧✧✧

"I really don't know if I could've raised my kids without a bathtub! I am really not joking. The bathtub saved me, and them, from times when they were bored, anxious, upset, and overtired. The sound of the water calmed them down (at all ages), and the warmth of the water helped them relax. I put tons of things in the bathtub for them to play with: plastic measuring cups, wooden spoons, plastic containers, army men, plastic animals, a beach pail and shovel, a colander...you name it! I found they became bored with commercial bath toys. I got creative with what I gave them to play with and they spent a lot of time, using their imaginations, in the bathtub. Whoever invented bathtubs, I thank you!"

—Alicia, Virginia Beach, Virginia

YOUNGER KIDS

SHOW them the pictures in a magazine or in a wordless book as they sit in the tub. Point out the objects in the picture and keep them interested by using your voice, pace, body language, and eye contact. Kids engage with engaging readers!

ASK them things like, "Where is the soap?" "There is it!" "Where is the shampoo?" "There it is!" "Where is the facecloth?" "There it is!" "Where is the potty?" "There it is!" "Where is the water?" "There it is!"

TEACH them how to blow bubbles in the bathtub. Bubbles are FUN and kids like FUN!

OLDER KIDS

SHOW them how to clean a bathtub. It's surprising how many kids don't give it a second thought. They think the water is enough to clean the tub. Surprise!

ASK them questions that will lead them to think about what THEY like and need. For instance, you might say, "Do you like to take baths or showers?" "Would you rather use liquid soap in a dispenser or soap in a box?" "What's your favorite time of day to take a shower or a bath?" "Why do you think people find baths and showers relaxing?"

TEACH them different ways they can stretch their bodies while they are in the shower. Many kids do not know how to STRETCH...too much sitting. You can suggest movements such as touching their toes and then holding that position, twisting to the left and to right as far as they can twist, raising both arms up to the ceiling with fingers spread wide, squatting down to stretch the lower spine, or touching their chin to their chest while the water comes down on their neck. There are lots of great ways to stretch the body in the tub or shower.

DINNER TABLE

"Every time we asked our kids about their day or about school, we always got one word answers like "good" or "nothing happened" or "fine." So we decided to try something we saw in a movie once. We told the kids that every night at dinner we were going to play "HIGH-LOW." The way you play is by telling one thing that happened in the day that made you feel really good, a HIGH...and one thing that happened that made you feel not-so-good, a LOW. At first the kids couldn't come up with much to say for each category, but after they heard our HIGHS and LOWS, they started to catch on. It took about 3 weeks and then it was fun and easy. We found ourselves thinking more about each day so that we could determine what made us feel good and not-so-good that day...and it brought us together as a family. We learned more about each other in that quick little around-the-table exchange, than we did at any other time. Try it!"

—Richard, San Diego, CA

YOUNGER KIDS

SHOW them the names of the items on the table as you point (together) to the placemats or table cloth, plates, forks, knives, napkins, spoons, salt and pepper shakers, glasses, and anything else on the table.

ASK them questions to help them identify and name things at the table. For instance, you might say, "Can you show me the spoon? Here it is!" "Can you show me the napkin? Here it is!" "Can you show me your banana? Here it is!" "Can you show me your cup? Here it is!" If they say "yes" and identify the wrong item, just point or hold it up for them and say, "Here it is." They will get the idea soon.

TEACH them how to count using peas, cheerios, grapes, blueberries, small cookies, animal crackers, macaroni, hot dog pieces, or apple slices. Whatever can be counted, count!

OLDER KIDS

SHOW them how to place the fork on the left and the knife on the right of a dinner plate. Show them how to place the glass to the top right of the place and the napkin to the left of the fork. As you do this, you will want to reinforce the concept of left and right. You would be surprised how many 'older kids' are still confused by left and right.

ASK them questions that will make them think about good nutrition and wholesome foods. For example, "What are the names of different kinds of meat that we could choose for our meals?" do the same for vegetables/pasta/bread/dairy/fruit/condiments. Then ask, "How many of each should we choose to have on our plate when we eat breakfast, lunch, and dinner?"

TEACH them how to eat slowly. That simple, that important!

GARAGE

◇◇◇◇◇◇◇◇◇◇◇◇◇◇◇◇◇◇◇◇

Especially for Dads: *Kids are naturally curious about machines and the way they work. Can you show and explain the inner workings (along with caution) of a lawn mower, snow blower, or weed whacker, perhaps? If not, how about lifting the hood of the car and showing kids what's under that hood? Fascinating!*

Especially for Moms: *What's the recycle bin for? Kids can help find stuff to go in it. Make a list of items that you use on regularly that can be recycled. Look up the word 'recycle' in the dictionary and discuss the importance of recycling so they understand why some things are recycled and not placed in the regular kitchen trash can.*

YOUNGER KIDS

SHOW them what's in the garage and have them name the items as you go 'on tour.' For example, have them point and say, "garage door" or "trash can" or "lawn mower." Build vocabulary!

ASK them things like, "Where is the door?" Then have them show you. "Where is the trash can?" "Where is the lawn mower?" Have them say the word as they show you.

TEACH them the concept of UP and DOWN or OPEN and CLOSE with the doors in your garage. Demonstrate. Say those words. Have them say them as the doors go up and door or open and close.

OLDER KIDS

SHOW them how to find tools in the garage. If there aren't any tools in your garage, make a list of all the tools that some people have in a garage. You can read them a book about tools or show them a website or catalog about tools. Kids love tools!

ASK them questions that will get them thinking about how things should be arranged in a garage after you draw a big rectangular or square box that represents a garage. You might ask, "Where do you think people should put the trash cans? Why?" They can actually draw them where they think they should go. "Why do you think people hang tools on the walls?" "Where is the best place for big equipment like a snow-blower, a ladder, or a lawn mower? Why do you think so?"

TEACH them how to sweep out a garage. Where should they start? What kind of broom is best? What do they do with the stuff they sweep up? Sweeping is a good thing to learn. They can do it!

KITCHEN

"Lots of livin' happens in a kitchen! I remember looking out the window on the day my daughter got her license. She was dying to take the car to the store by herself. I watched her get into the car and she smiled at me as she waved. As she put the car in reverse and headed down the driveway and onto the street, I was overcome with flashbacks of the main events in her life. They all appeared like I was watching a movie. I got hysterical as I sunk onto the kitchen floor and prayed that she would be safe every time she got into a car to drive. My husband came in and thought I was hurt. He wiped my face and said, "Hon, she's just going to CVS. She'll be right back! I said, "Ok." But in my heart, I knew she wasn't just going to CVS. She was going into adulthood."

—Mary, Bethlehem, PA

Younger Kids

SHOW them how to put fruits and vegetables in the refrigerator drawers. Have them say what they are and then have them count the apples, tomatoes, lemons, peaches, oranges, and peppers as they place them, one by one.

ASK them, "Where is the butter?" Show me. "Where is the lettuce?" Show me. "Where is the milk?" Show me. Then ask, "What sound does butter start with?" Say, "Bbbbb." "What sound does lettuce make?" Say, "Lllll." "What sound does "milk start with?" Say, "Mmmm." Keep this up!

TEACH them about letter, sounds, and words by placing magnetic letters on the refrigerator. Have them make words like Mom, Dad, yes, no, the. Have them show you letters that you name. Have them make words that rhyme: fun, run, sun or cat, rat, mat. Magnetic letters are magical. Use them!

OLDER KIDS

SHOW them how a refrigerator is organized. Have them help put away the groceries in the 'right place' and ask them if they think there is a better way to organize the refrigerator. They might have one!

ASK them questions that make them think such as, "How do you think the soap cleans the dishes in the dishwasher?" "Why is there a light in the oven and in the microwave?" "How does toast pop up in the toaster?" "What's the difference between the freezer and the refrigerator?"

TEACH them how to organize the silverware into categories, how to stack the dishwasher, and how to organize pots and pans. Kids need to be taught organizational skills. The kitchen is a perfect place for that.

LIVING ROOM

✧✧✧✧✧✧✧✧✧✧✧✧✧✧✧✧✧✧✧✧✧✧✧✧✧✧✧✧

Especially for Dads: *Kids are fascinated by the television remote control, from a very young age! Show them how it works and what the different buttons do. Show them where the batteries go and how they have a + and – side to them. Cool!*

Especially for Moms: *Show kids how to stack things. They are natural stackers and we Moms tend to like it when things are stacked. Have them stack pillows, magazines, logs for the fire, photo albums, books, coasters, and anything else that needs stacking.*

YOUNGER KIDS

SHOW them how to find things by hiding them around the living room. Say, "Where is the ball?" "There is the ball!" "Where is my shoe?" "There is my shoe!" "Where is the teddy bear?" "There is the teddy bear!"

ASK them things that will require them to follow oral directions. For example, "Can you put the pillow on the couch?" "Can you put my slippers under the coffee table?" "Can you find something soft?" "Can you find something green?"

TEACH them how to roll a ball by sitting across from each other on the living room floor with legs spread out like a big 'V.' Then push the ball towards them as you say, "Push." Now have them push the ball back as they say, "Push." Go back and forth like this. Fun!

OLDER KIDS

SHOW them how to vacuum the living room. They are curious about vacuum cleaners. Let them see how it works and where the dirt goes. Show them how to vacuum ceiling corners…that's neat!

ASK them questions that will help them think about 'living spaces' such as, "Why do you think this room is called a living room?" "Do you think all houses have the same number of rooms in them?" "What rooms do you think a house or apartment HAS to have?" "What kind of place do you want to live in someday and what would it look like?"

TEACH them how to play 'charades.' Act out an action and have them guess what you're doing. Then let them have a turn. Keep going. This game is easy, inexpensive, and it helps kids think!

PORCH

◇◇◇◇◇◇◇◇◇◇◇◇◇

Especially for Dads: *Show kids how a porch is built. Perhaps you could explain how it is attached to a house, how the porch floor can support people and furniture, or how the front porch steps are connected. 'This old porch…'*
Especially for Moms: *Have an old fashioned 'tea party' or a lemonade stand on a front porch. Give kids practice with making, setting up, serving, and selling tea or lemonade. Summer fun!*

YOUNGER KIDS

SHOW them how to move across a porch with BIG steps and SMALL steps, counting as they go. Show them how to walk forwards and backwards and how to hop, jump, and skip on a porch. It's a great place to move!

ASK them what they see while they are on a porch. For example, "Can you see a tree? Show me." "Can you see the sky?" Show me." "Can you see the door? Show me?" "Can you see your shoe? Show me."

TEACH them how to read a book with no words (wordless book) as you sit on a porch together. You will want to model this by talking about the pictures in detail and by pointing out things that you notice on each page. Pictures speak a thousand words. Teach them how!

OLDER KIDS

SHOW them how to do a puzzle while on the porch. There isn't much to do on a porch. A puzzle will catch their eye and give them something to engage with. Many kids do not know HOW to go about putting together a puzzle.

ASK them things like, "Do you think it would be easier to start with the outside pieces or the inside pieces of this puzzle? Why do you think so?" "Why do people use the puzzle box cover to help them?" "What do you think we should do if we get stuck on one part of the puzzle?"

TEACH them how to create things with some glue, toothpicks, pipe cleaners, Q-tips, popsicle sticks, cotton balls, play-dough, or cheerios. Creating something is good for the soul...and the attention span.

STAIRS

◇◇◇◇◇◇◇◇◇◇◇◇◇

"One day I saw my baby son crawling towards the stairs. I stayed back and just watched to see what he would do. When he got to the stairs, he paused and looked up. Then, he just turned and headed in another direction as fast as he could! I couldn't help thinking that life is like that. If we look at all the stairs at once, we may not want to try at all. Eventually, my son took it 'one step at a time' until he was running up and down the staircase easily and swiftly."

—Ron, North Tonawanda, NY

YOUNGER KIDS

SHOW them how to count forwards and backwards as you climb up and down the stairs. Go fast and go slow as you count quickly and slowly. You can also skip stairs and count by two's, but be careful!

ASK them questions about colors while sitting on the stairs together. For example, you might ask, "What color is the sun?" "What color is a carrot?" "What color is milk?" "What color is the sky?" "What color is snow?" "What color is the grass?" "What color is an egg?" "Now which ones were white? Let's see…milk, snow, and an egg!"

TEACH them how to repeat the number of times you clap, while you're hanging out on the stairs one day. For instance, you clap fast, 3 times, and they have to clap fast, 3 times. You clap once, then two times fast, then once again. They have to copy that. This is SO good for listening skills. Clap on stairs!

OLDER KIDS

SHOW them how to measure the width, height, and depth of a step on the house staircase (or any steps that are available) with a tape measure, ruler, yardstick, or all three.

ASK them to tell you what they found out by measuring the step. "How wide is each step?" "How high is it?" How deep is each step from the front to the back?" "How wide do you think they should be, or are they just right?"

TEACH them how to count by 2s, 3s, 5s, 10s, and 20s as you go up and down a flight of stairs. Go fast, go slow, count fast, count slow. This will help with multiplication facts! Climb and count, climb and count.

YARD

<><><><><><><><><>

A neighborhood boy came over to visit me while I was watering my flowers. He wanted to help me. Since I am a teacher, I figured I would catch 'the teachable minute.' So I taught him what categories are by having him water the flowers according to color, size, shape, and height. When he left, he knew what a 'category' was…and my flowers were grateful!

—Ashley, Choctaw, OK

Especially for Dads: *Take kids to a hardware store and show them all the tools that are made just for people's yards. For instance, a rake, hose, birdfeeder, birdhouse, sprinkler, shovel, wheelbarrow, fertilizer spreader, outdoor thermometer, hammock, lawn mower, hedge trimmer, clippers, etc. Even if you don't have a yard, kids could benefit from knowing what these are and what they do.*

Especially for Moms: *Show kids how plant tulip and daffodil bulbs in the autumn. They will love digging holes and stuffing big fat bulbs into them. If you don't have a yard, you can do this in a big bucket or a large planter. They will be amazed when they pop up in the spring.*

YOUNGER KIDS

SHOW them how to pick up sticks, pull out weeds, feed the birds, and water the grass. They will surprise you!

ASK them things like, "Why do squirrels bury nuts?" "Why do birds come to the birdfeeder?" "How come people have to water grass and flowers?" "What makes flowers grow?"

TEACH them how to play "Simon Says" outside in the yard. You say, "Simon Says jump up and down." They jump up and down. "Simon says walk 3 steps." They walk 3 steps. "Now run to that tree." They should not run to the tree because you didn't say, "Simon Says." Great game for learning how to follow oral directions…and it's a lot of fun!

OLDER KIDS

SHOW them how to mow the lawn, rake the leaves, and water the grass. They don't have to do it perfectly, just do it!

ASK them questions that help them think about what they might do in certain situations while you sit in the yard together. For example, "What would you do if you saw a squirrel in our house?" "What would you do if you were walking home from school and you saw lightning in the sky?" "What should we do if there's a tornado coming towards our town?"

TEACH them how to take pictures when you're in a yard together. What do kids need to know about taking pictures? What are all the different ways they could take a picture of the same scene or the same object outside? Kids love to take pictures, but many of them don't know how.

PUBLIC
PLACES

A public place is merely a garden for kids to grow.

PLANT IDEAS…

For more information on how to
PLANT IDEAS with your kids visit:
theteachableminute.com/plant

AIRPORT

◇◇◇◇◇◇◇◇◇◇◇◇◇◇◇◇◇◇

Especially for Dads: *Kids love birds and planes! Make the comparison for kids next time you're at the airport. Then tell them about all the different parts of a plane so they understand how it works and learn new words at the same time.*

Especially for Moms: *The airport is a great place to read books to kids, to show them things they don't see every day, and to teach them about the importance of informational signs of all kinds. Why not do all three?!*

YOUNGER KIDS

SHOW them how to drink from a water fountain, wash their hands in a public restroom, and wait in line patiently. These are all things that must be taught.

ASK questions that will make them think, depending on their age. Here are some examples you might try: "Why do people go on airplanes?" "Is an airplane the same as a car?" "Where do you think our suitcases go on the plane?" "Can a car go faster than a plane?" "Who is the pilot?"

TEACH them new words by pointing out things in an airport that are new to them, such as a suitcase, runway, wheelchair, taxi, kiosk, cash register, water fountain, exit sign, elevator, moving walkway, and jet-way. Lots of new words!

OLDER KIDS

SHOW them how to find the city they are going to, pointing out how they are alphabetized so that they can be found easily. Call out the names of other cities and show them how to find them quickly and easily. Be sure they notice the gate number and departure times.

ASK them things like, "How many different kinds of planes do you think there are?" Let's look that up and see. "What do you think gets the plane off the ground?" "Why did it have to speed up so much in order to take off?" "Why do you think the pilot can't make the plane move backwards like we can in our car?" Let's look these things up in a book or on the internet.

TEACH them how to read and understand what is on an airline boarding pass. Where is the flight number located on it? How do you know where you are going and when? Where is the seat number listed? Why does everyone need a boarding pass to get on the plane?

APARTMENT COMPLEX

"I guess you could say that I caught the teachable minute after our son move into his first apartment. One day he sent me a text message that read, "Hey, Mom. Hope you and Dad are well. How do you make those cheese blintz things you make at Thanksgiving?" I smiled and sent him the recipe. Guess he still needs me!
—Martha, Kennebunkport, ME

YOUNGER KIDS

SHOW them what an apartment complex looks like and point out how it is different than a neighborhood of houses. Build their vocabulary by pointing to the pool, the office, the parking lot, the mailboxes, the doors and windows, and the trash bins.

ASK them questions that will help them think about where people and animals live. "Where does Grandpa live?" "Where do horses live?" "Where do birds live?" "Where do squirrels live?" "Where do dogs and cats live?" "Where do fish live?"

TEACH them how to count the cars, doors, mailboxes, or sidewalk squares in an apartment complex. Count whatever can be counted!

OLDER KIDS

SHOW them the floor plan of an apartment or draw one for them. Compare it to a house floor plan, a library floor plan, and an office building floor plan. How are they are the same and how are they different?

ASK questions that lead to critical thinking such as, "Why do you think apartment buildings were invented?" "Why would someone want to live in an apartment and not in a house?" "What would you do if the fire alarm went off in a high floor apartment and the elevators weren't working?" "Why do you think that big cities have more apartment buildings than towns do?"

TEACH them how to find apartments for rent, houses for sale, and jobs available either in the paper or on the internet. What information should they be noticing when they look at ads? Kids need to know these things.

BOOKSTORE

Especially for Dads: *Find the section in a bookstore where kids can look at maps and an atlas with you. What do they need to know? How can you help them understand how to 'read' these important informational texts?*

Especially for Moms: *There's an old saying that goes like this: "You can't judge a book by its cover." But, the fact is that kids are drawn to books because of their covers, in many instances. Show them lots of different book covers. Help them understand what they can learn about the book from its cover. You an even have them draw their own design for a book cover. Book covers are neat!*

YOUNGER KIDS

SHOW them big books, little book, fat books, skinny books, silly books, board books, cloth books, and any other kinds of books you can find in a bookstore. Let them hold them, turn the pages in them, and point to things they see on the pages. Book handling skills are important.

ASK them "DO YOU SEE" questions. For instance, "Do you see a boy in this book? Show me." "Do you see a bird on the front of this book? Show me." "Do you see a baby on the back of this book? Show me." "Do you see a truck on page 3? Show me."

TEACH them how to find the page number on each page and how to say the number as they point to it and turn the page.

OLDER KIDS

SHOW them how a bookstore is organized into specific sections and how books are organized into categories that are labeled on large signs above the shelves. If you prefer to search an internet bookstore, you will want to show them how to search difference categories for books they may be interested in.

ASK them questions that check on their understandings of what is inside a book. For instance, have them to show you the title page. Then ask, "Why does a book need a title page?" Have them show you the Table of Contents and/or the Index. Then ask, "Why do these pages help us?" Have them show you the book cover or book jacket. Then ask, "What are all the things we can learn about a book from the cover or jacket?"

TEACH them how to find specific book titles or books by specific authors using the bookstore's computer or on the internet in the 'search' bar. Tap into areas that they are interested in. For instance, if they like baseball, have them search for an autobiography of a famous baseball player.

CEMETERY

◇◇◇◇◇◇◇◇◇◇◇◇◇◇◇◇◇◇◇◇◇◇◇

Our first house was on a street that was only two streets away from a large cemetery. Our kids would often ride their bikes with the neighborhood kids through the cemetery. One night our neighbor's daughter came over to say, "Don't be afraid of the cemetery. When you see it, close your eyes, hold your breath and puff out your cheeks. Then say, 'THE CEMETERY,' out loud slowly and you will have good luck!" To this day, I think we all still do what she told us, for good luck of course!

—Meghan, West Springfield, MA

YOUNGER KIDS

SHOW them the different types of tombstones that are found in a cemetery. Kids are fascinated by them and they will not be afraid of these places if they are shown at a young age.

ASK them if they know how to find certain letters and numbers on tombstones. "Can you show me an uppercase M for Michael?" "Can you show me the number 1, the number 6, and the number 5?" "Can you show me a name that starts like your name?" Eventually they will learn that names and dates are written on tombstones and they will be able to read them.

TEACH them whatever you feel is important to their understanding of what a cemetery is and why we have them. The idea is to help them not be afraid when they visit or hear about a cemetery.

OLDER KIDS

SHOW them different kinds of cemeteries around the world either in a book or on the internet. How do different cultures bury the dead? What are the different tombstones that are used to identify people?

ASK them questions that help them process the concept of cemeteries. For instance, "Why do you think people put flowers, flags, angels, and other things at grave sites?" "What could we do if we wanted to find the grave site of someone in our family who died long ago?" "What information can be found on most tombstones?"

TEACH kids a variety of ways that we show compassion for those who lose family members, friends and pets. There are many books that can help children understand 'death' and how to cope with it. Visiting a cemetery with you helps kids feel safe and secure when they see one or have to go to one.

COLLEGE CAMPUS

Especially for Dads: *Many kids never get the chance to see what a college looks like until they are really big kids. Consider taking them to a campus to show them how it's like a little town. If they have never seen what a college looks like, how will they really know if they want to go?*

Especially for Moms: *Ask this very important question when you are alone with your son or daughter: "What can you do best that you like and is easy for you to do?" If they don't know, wait. Keep asking, every now and then, until they come up with it on their own. It is SO important that kids know what they are naturally good at before they decide what they want to do with their lives.*

YOUNGER KIDS

SHOW them around a college campus so they will know it is a safe place. Build vocabulary by pointing out things like: building, sidewalk, parking lot, windows, flowers, trees, grass, books, library, tennis courts, football field, bleachers, and dormitory. Don't hesitate to use big words!

ASK questions like, "Where are all the kids going?" "Why do kids go to the library?" "When do the kids go home?" "Why do kids sleep here?"

TEACH them how to throw and catch a 'squishy' football. Throwing and catching build eye-hand coordination. Build it!

OLDER KIDS

SHOW them how to read a map or directory of the campus. Ask them in which direction they would go, to get to the campus bookstore, the pool, the library, and the food hall. Mapping skills are important...and no, they can't use a GPS for this!

ASK questions about how they would handle 'sticky' situations. For instance, "What would you do if you hurt yourself?" "What might you say to kids in your dorm if you have an exam the next day and they are making noise late at night?" "How would you approach your professor if you feel you get an unfair grade on a project or paper?"

TEACH them how to protect themselves in a parking lot if they feel someone is watching or following them, especially at night. One way is to start walking faster, wave in the direction of their car or dormitory, and call out, "Hey, I'm coming. How are you doing?" Anyone who is following them will think that there are people around and they will 'bug out' fast. This works!

CLOTHING STORE

"Talk about the teachable minute... I caught one when my 6-year-old and I were shopping for school clothes. The baby was in the stroller and I let my 6-year-old walk next to me 'like a big boy." Big mistake. I told him to hold onto the stroller while I looked through the rack of boy's pants and shirts. He did, but in one second, I looked down and he was gone. I knew he couldn't have gone far and I started calling him. My heart quickly found its way up to the throat and my voice got louder and louder. The tears were instant. The panic was frightening. Suddenly, he jumped out from under the clothes on the rack and shouted, "Here I am, Mom." I immediately hugged him while I sobbed. And then, I explained why he could NEVER do that to me, or anyone else again. I handled it well, but I grew about 10 gray hairs that day."

—Jennifer, Denver, CO

YOUNGER KIDS

SHOW them all the different types of clothing that is available in the store. Hold up items and tell them what they are. Encourage them to repeat the label as you show them. For instance, hold up a jacket and say, "Jacket." Then say, "What is this?" Keep at it. They are listening even if they don't want to talk. It is sinking in.

ASK questions that help them think about what they like and don't like. Hold up a shirt or pants and ask, "Do you like this color or this color?" You may have to wait for the answer. Wait time is important. "Do you like these mittens or these gloves?" "Do you like this jacket with buttons or this one with a zipper?" Kids feel special and important when they are offered CHOICES.

TEACH them how to look at the tags on clothes and to find their size. Point out numbers on the tag until they can find the size themselves. Kids love tags!

OLDER KIDS

SHOW them large signs around a store that can help us find things. Kids need to learn to read signs so they can find things quickly and easily.

ASK questions such as, "What do you want to look for first?" "What is the most important thing we need to come home with?" "Where should we look if we find these clothes are too expensive?" "When you get dressed for school, what kind of clothes do you wish you had more of?" "How much money do we have to spend today?" Put the responsibility on them as you guide them to plan ahead. Many kids do not know how to prioritize what they need (and don't need) when they go shopping.

TEACH them how to shop wisely by creating scenarios for them to think about. Say, "If 3 pairs of socks costs $16.00 or one pair costs $10.00, which is a better deal?" or "Why do you think this jacket is a better value than that jacket?" "Should we get 3 ties that you may not wear just because the sale sign says, Buy Two, Get One Free?"

CONVENIENCE STORE

Especially for Dads: *Kids can learn a lot from the way things are packaged. While you're in the store together, show them the information that can be found on candy bar labels, soda cans, potato chip bags, cereal boxes, bottled water bottles, and anything else you can find.*
Especially for Moms: *What can a dollar buy these days? Help kids find things in the store that will up to (or just below) $1.00. This will teach them how to make choices and to stay within a given amount. Do the same with $2.00 and with $5.00. See what they come up with. Have pen and paper or a phone calculator with you so you can add things up together.*

YOUNGER KIDS

SHOW kids different items that are stacked on shelves and in refrigerators at a convenience store or small corner market. Hold up items and name them. Do this with babies as well. Do not underestimate them just because they cannot talk yet. They are taking it all in. Keep at it.

ASK questions that help kids learn their letters and sounds. For instance, "Can you show me something on the shelf that starts with a B?" "Where do you see the first letter of your name on this box? Show me." "What letter does SODA start with?" "What letter does MILK start with?" "Can you show me the M for MAN on the restroom door?" "What other words start like 'man'?

TEACH them how to find prices on the things you want to buy. Once they find the price, tell them how much the item costs. They will learn to look for the prices of things if you do this often.

OLDER KIDS

SHOW kids features of a convenience store that make it convenient! Point out the gas pumps, bagged ice bin, lottery tickets, and general products. Talk about why we have these stores everywhere and why we don't we just go to big super markets? Discuss the reasons why things are more expensive in these stores or why these stores don't sell items like steak, chicken, watermelon, or spinach.

ASK questions that help kids to search for information on product labels. You might ask, "How many calories are in that soda?" "Where does that bottled water come from?" "What ingredients are in those potato chips?" "Is there any sodium in that bottle of milk? How do you know?"

TEACH kids how to check a receipt for the items you purchased. Help them understand the following: Why do we get receipts for things we buy? What should we look for to be sure things add up correctly? What information is found on a receipt? Receipts are part of our modern world.

DENTAL OFFICE

"We had just watched the movie, Mary Poppins,® a few days before our son went to the dentist for his check-up. After the dentist checked his teeth, he looked up at Jimmy and asked, "Have you been eating a lot of sugar, boy?" Jimmy looked him right in the eye and proudly said, "Yes, Sir. I had a bad cough and just a spoon full of sugar makes the medicine go down. Ya know?" Our dentist said that was the first time he had ever heard that line…and it was a good one!"

—Luisa, San Antonio, TX

YOUNGER KIDS

SHOW young kids some books from the library or the bookstore about going to the dentist. This will help them know what to expect and they may not feel as anxious when they are there.

ASK questions that can help them learn more about taking care of their teeth. For example, "Why do people have to brush their teeth every morning and every night?" "Why do so many people lose their teeth when they are older?" "Why do we have to use dental floss once a day?"

TEACH them the difference between good brushing and bad brushing. Show them the right way and the wrong way. Then they will know for sure.

OLDER KIDS

SHOW kids all the different kinds of toothbrushes that are available at the store. Point out features that make them different. Let them select one that looks like it will be best for their teeth. Do the same with toothpaste and dental floss. Let kids choose and they will use!

ASK questions that help them think making good food choices. Offer choices for them to consider after asking the question, "What's better for your teeth? Marshmallows or grapes? A lollipop or ice cream? An apple or a cookie? Chocolate milk or white milk? A candy bar or a granola bar? Orange juice or soda?" They may have to look up the sugar content in some of those!

TEACH kids how to floss their teeth in front of a mirror. Many kids don't see the point or the value of taking time to floss their teeth once a day. Many of them think that brushing is all they need to do. Clue them in!

DRIVE-IN THEATER

Especially for Grandparents: What would kids like to know about drive-in theaters? There aren't many around today. Can you draw a picture of what they looked like and tell them how we were able to hear the movie's sound? Stories help kids learn how to speak well...tell them all you can!

YOUNGER KIDS

SHOW them pictures of a drive-in movie theater in a book or on the internet. Point out things that can be found at a drive-in movie theater such as big screen, big parking lot, many cars, lots of speakers, and popcorn!

ASK questions to build phonemic awareness like, "What sound does DRIVE start with?" "What 2 sounds does THEATER start with?" "What is your tongue doing when you say words like THEATER, THINK, THANK, THAT?" "What sound does MOVIE start with?" "What other words start with the 'M' sound?" "What words end with the 'th' sound?" "What words end with 'm'?"

TEACH them how to draw a big square like the shape of a movie screen or a big parking lot. Make lots of squares. Draw big squares, little squares, fat squares, tiny squares, and even silly squares.

OLDER KIDS

SHOW them what a drive-in movie theater looks like. Show them how it was set up so that lots of people could see one movie, all from the inside of their cars. Cool!

ASK them questions that will get them to think about managing such a place. "What would you charge people to see the movie if you owned a drive-in theater?" "Do you think your expenses would be more or less than an inside theater would be?" "Why do you think so?" "How many people do you think you would have to hire to run it?" "What do you think the biggest problem with owning a drive-in theater is?"

TEACH them how to make change. Have them pretend they are working at the drive-in snack bar. Create scenarios such as, if an ice cream cone costs $3.75 and I give you $5.00, how much change should you give me back? If a large bag of popcorn costs $5.25 and I give you $20.00, how much will I get back? Use real bills and coins. Help them learn how to calculate in their heads, without a calculator or cash register.

ELEVATOR

Especially for Dads: *What makes an elevator go up and down? How does it know to stop at certain floors? Most kids are both fascinated and scared when they get into an elevator. How can you help them learn how it works?*

Especially for Moms: *Kids need to know how to behave on an elevator. What can you tell them so they don't get hurt and so they are respectful of others while riding on the elevator?*

YOUNGER KIDS

SHOW them the numbers on the elevator buttons. Point and count to each one. Let them push the button for the floor you need to go to. While you are riding the elevator, use words like push, up, down, open, and close. Important words to know!

ASK things like, "Are we going up?" "Is it time to go?" "Is the door opened?" "Are we going down?" "Is the door closed?" "Is the door opened or closed?"

TEACH kids how to wait their turn when they get on and off of an elevator. This will teach them to be aware of others while in a crowded space.

OLDER KIDS

SHOW books or videos about elevators so they learn how they work and what makes them 'stop' and 'go.'

ASK a few good questions about safety. For instance, "What would you do if the elevator suddenly stopped in between floors?" "Why do you think people can't take an elevator when there is a fire in the building?" "What would you do if the elevator door started to close while you were getting in it?"

TEACH them about the history of elevators by looking up facts about when they were invented and how they changed over time. Can they find out who originally thought of making an elevator? Ask them if they have any ideas on how to make elevators work faster and better. Bet they do!

ESCALATOR

◇◇◇◇◇◇◇◇◇◇◇◇◇◇◇◇◇◇◇◇◇◇◇

"My 'teachable minute' appeared when my 3 kids and I were getting on an escalator together one day at the airport. Lots of people were climbing the escalator, obviously in a hurry. The kids were watching people run up and down the escalators. When we got off, they looked confused. My youngest said, "Mom, there are lots of people who think they have to climb up and down the steps to make it go. Someone should tell them!" I took the time to explain to her why the steps don't work that way and why some people choose to walk while others stand still."

—Karen, Longmeadow, MA

YOUNGER KIDS

SHOW kids HOW to get on and off an escalator instead of just taking their hand and 'pulling' them along. They will learn quickly how to hold onto the rail and to move quickly!

ASK questions about how they feel when they are on an escalator. For example, "Do you like escalators?" "Do you like when it goes UP or when it goes DOWN best?" "Do you think dogs can go on escalators?" "What would we do if the escalator stopped? How would we get off?"

TEACH them how many syllables (parts) are in the word, ES-CA-LA-TOR. Show them how to jump or stomp each part of the word as they say it slowly. Then invite them to do it with you in different ways. Try tapping the word on the table with your elbow. Try blinking it or bobbing your head. Try raising a finger for each part of the word…altogether, there should be 4 fingers standing tall. Hearing syllables in words helps kids when they write hard words.

OLDER KIDS

SHOW them how a book or video about how an escalator works. Kids are naturally curious and they will be grateful to know how this thing moves up and down.

ASK questions that help kids wonder. "Why do you think stores and airports use escalators instead of stairs?" "When do you think people thought of this idea?" "What would happen if all the escalators and elevators in an airport or a skyscraper shut down for a day?" "How could we find out where the longest escalator in the world is?"

TEACH kids how look up escalator in the dictionary or on Wikipedia. What are all the things they can learn about one word by looking it up? Lots of kids don't know how great a teacher a dictionary can be!

EYE DOCTOR'S OFFICE

Especially for Dads: *How does 'the eye' really work? What makes us 'see'? Why do eyeglasses help people see well? Kids would love to know.*
Especially for Moms: *Lots of kids wear glasses, but they often lose them and don't know how to care for them properly. Show them how to rinse them with warm water and liquid soap. Establish one place where they should put their glasses when they aren't wearing them. This will save time and money!*

YOUNGER KIDS

SHOW them a book about going to the eye doctor before they go. This will reduce anxiety and help them to know what to expect.

ASK questions that help them get use to answering questions about their eyes. For instance, "Do your eyes hurt you when you read a book?" "Do you have to rub your eyes a lot?" "How do your eyes feel when you look at a sign that's far away?" "Do you know any kids who wear glasses?" "What color are your eyes?"

TEACH them new and different words while you are waiting to see the doctor such as, waiting room, magazines, eye chart, equipment, examining room, big chair, flashlight, etc.

OLDER KIDS

SHOW them all the different kinds of eyeglass frames that are available. Even if they don't wear glasses, kids like to try them on and see which ones look good on them!

ASK them things like, "Why do you think someone would want to become an eye doctor?" "Why do you think the letters and numbers on an eye chart get smaller and smaller?" "What would be the best thing about being an eye doctor?" "Why do you think bifocal lenses were invented?" Good things for them to investigate if they don't know the answers.

TEACH them the difference between an ophthalmologist and an optometrist. Teach them how to hear the sounds in those words and how to write them, too. Lots of kids don't use hard words when they write because they don't know how to 'chunk them' into small bites.

FIRE STATION

◇◇◇◇◇◇◇◇◇◇◇◇◇◇◇◇◇◇◇◇◇◇◇◇◇◇◇◇◇

"My 2 little guys love to visit their Dad at the fire station. One day, I walked into the station to pick them up and they said, "Watch this, Mom." One of them was upstairs at the top of the fire pole while the other was stationed at the bottom of the pole. The next thing I heard was, "C'mon, Buddy. You can do it!" Would you believe that they taught our puppy how to hold on with all four of his legs and come down the pole? I screamed and they clapped. "Don't worry, Mom. We taught him how!" Could there be the teachable minute for dogs, too? I guess so!"
—Linda, Banff, Canada

YOUNGER KIDS

SHOW kids what a fire extinguisher and a fire alarm look like. Lots of kids see these things around, but don't know what they are for. Tell them why they need to learn to pay attention when the fire alarm comes on.

ASK questions on the way to or from the fire station that will stretch their thinking. For instance, "How is a fire fighter different from a police officer?" "What equipment does a fire fighter need?" "Why do fire fighters and police officers have to sleep at the station sometimes?" "What number do we call on our phone when we need help?" "How do fire fighters get to a burning house so fast?" "Would you like to be a fire fighter?" "Why or why not?"

TEACH them about the different things they see on a fire truck and what each thing does. Examples might be: the hose, ladder, bell, back door, fire suit, mask, and ax.

OLDER KIDS

SHOW kids where the fire station is located in your town or city. Talk with them about why people might choose to become a fire fighter for a job. What are the pros and cons?

ASK them things like, "What kind of training do you think fire fighters have to get before they can go out on a fire call?" "Do you think it would be easier to be a fire fighter in a town or in a city? Why?" "What's a fire hydrant for?"

TEACH them how to come up with a list of questions they would ask a fire fighter if they were going to interview them at the fire station. Start with what the most important thing is that they want and need to know.

FLOWER SHOP

Especially for Grandparents: Teach beauty. As we get older, it seems that we appreciate the simple things more. Kids will remember what you teach them and share with them. Flowers make the world simply beautiful!

YOUNGER KIDS

SHOW them all the different flowers that are in the 'glass refrigerator' at the flower shop. Can they name the colors? Can they pick out their favorite one?

ASK questions that will get kids thinking about why we do things for others. For instance, you might ask, "Why do people give other people flowers?" "What would you do if you wanted to give your friend a flower and you didn't have any money?" "When do you people smile when we give them a flower?" "If you grew a beautiful flower, who would you give it to?"

TEACH the names of flowers. The more they know, the smarter they will be!

OLDER KIDS

SHOW them the florist's book of floral arrangements. Let them search for the ones they like the best for weddings, funerals, Mother's Day, and holidays. Who knew there were so many ways of arranging flowers?

ASK them questions that will help them think about what it takes to own a shop like this. For instance, "Why do you think someone goes into the floral business?" "Where do they get the flowers?" "How many people do you think they have to hire?" "What does a florist have to know about flowers?" "How do they get the money to open a shop like this?"

TEACH them how to choose and fill out the right 'gift card' that would go with a flower arrangement. Ask them which card they would choose for a wedding, funeral, and sickness. Kids don't automatically know these things!

FUNERAL HOME

"My 'teachable minute' came when my daughter wiped my tears from my face and said, "Mommy, why are you crying? Grandma has so many flowers now." Precious…

—Grace, Baton Rouge, LA

YOUNGER KIDS

SHOW them what a funeral home looks like. You can find photos in books or on the internet. Kids tend to feel better when they know what places like funeral homes, hospitals, schools, medical offices, and airports look like before they go. Pictures do speak a thousand words!

ASK them things that help them keep a visit to a funeral home light and easy. For instance, you might ask them to find people and things they know. Ask things like, "Do you see your cousin? Where is he?" "Do you see your brother/sister?" "Do you see lots of flowers?" "Do you see lots of chairs?" "Do you see Daddy/Mommy?"

TEACH them how to be respectful of those who mourn. They will learn quickly. Kids are naturally compassionate.

OLDER KIDS

SHOW them pictures of the deceased so they will know who they have come to pay their respects to.

ASK questions that help them process what is happening. You might ask, "Why do people come here?" "Why do many people bring flowers?" "What do the people who work for funeral homes do?" "Why do people sign a book when they get here?" "Do you think all funerals around the world are the same?" "Do you have any questions about what happens in a funeral home?" Pick and choose your questions. They are offered only as a way to deal with fear and anxiety, if the teachable minute presents itself.

TEACH them what to say to people who are with them at a funeral. You might suggest some phrases that are appropriate and heartfelt. For example, "I am so sorry to hear of your loss." "Is there anything you need?" "Thank you for having me" or simply, "I know you will miss him/her." Kids don't really know what to say in situations like this. Practice with them.

HOSPITAL

~~~~~~~~~~~~~~~~~~~~~~~~~~

Especially for Dads: *Take kids on a tour of a hospital just in case they ever have to go to a hospital. What can you tell them about the emergency room, an ambulance, and an operating room? Point out signs and directories that will guide them in finding where they need to go.*

Especially for Moms: *All kids love to visit the hospital baby nursery. Take them on a little tour. What do they need to know about this first 'baby experience'?!*

YOUNGER KIDS

SHOW kids what a wheelchair looks like and how it works. Explain why some people need them. Point out the parts on the wheelchair so they learn new words such as, wheel, spokes, handles, lever, and foot rest.

ASK questions that held kids think about the purpose of hospitals. "Why do people go to the hospital?" "What do nurses and doctors do at the hospital?" "Can people get medicine at a hospital?" "Why are there beds in a hospital?" "Why do we have to be quiet when we go to a hospital?" "What is the 'emergency room' for?" "Where do they keep the ambulance?"

TEACH them new words that are associated with hospitals such as illness, accident, operation, stethoscope, ambulance, shot, baby nursery, medicine, wheelchair, crutches, doctor, and nurse.

OLDER KIDS

SHOW kids a video or a book about emergency room care, the operating room, or an X-ray lab. Many kids are curious about these special places. If they ever have to be patients, they will know what to expect and this will reduce fear and anxiety.

ASK them things that will help expand their knowledge of what happens in a hospital. "Why do hospitals need X-ray technicians?" "Why do nurses take people's temperature and heart rate so often?" "Where do they send samples of patient's blood?" "What do doctors wear when they operate on patients?" "Why do nurses and doctors always wear gloves?" "What do you think you would like about having to be in a hospital overnight?" "What do you think you would not like?"

TEACH them how to read the directory and information signs when you visit a hospital together. What floor are certain departments located on? Where is the cafeteria or coffee shop? Where is the flower shop? Where are the exits?

HOTEL OR MOTEL

"When our kids were little, they loved to go to hotels and motels. One day, while we were coming back from the beach, I asked them why they liked them so much. Our oldest took the lead and said, "Dad, don't you know that it's because we can jump on the beds? Where else can we do that?!" I said, "Oh...I get it now." I wondered if I should've told them not to jump on those beds, but then I thought of the legs I use to have before we went to war. I decided to let them jump and jump and jump. Sometimes, you just gotta let the teachable minute pass on by... and catch another one later."

—Eric, Phoenix, AZ

YOUNGER KIDS

SHOW kids all the facilities at a hotel or motel, several times, so they learn the names of things. Examples would be the front desk, lobby, business office, coffee shop or gift shop, fitness center, restaurant, restrooms, meeting rooms, parking lot, yard, playground, and pool, of course!

ASK questions like, "Can you show me the pool? Point to it." "Can you show me the menu? Point to it." "Can you show me the television? Point to it." "Can you show me the alarm clock? Point to it." "Can you show me the name of the hotel? Point to it."

TEACH kids how to find room numbers. Have them count them as you walk down the hallways.

OLDER KIDS

SHOW kids how to find a listing of hotels and motels in a city on the internet or in a tour book. What information do they need to look for before choosing a place to stay?

ASK questions that lead kids to make comparisons. For instance you might say, "How are hotels and motels different?" "Why do we find more hotels in big cities than motels?" "Do you think it costs more to build a hotel or a motel?" "Why do you think motels usually have outside doors and parking spaces that are near the rooms?" "Why do you think someone designed hotels?" "What services do expensive hotels have that smaller hotels or motels don't have?"

TEACH them the proper way to call and ask for wake-up calls, food, late check-out times, and maintenance or internet service. Do they know how to use 'please' and 'thank you'? Important!

MALL

Especially for Dads: *Consider taking kids to stores that have sporting equipment. Show them how a treadmill works or how many different kinds of tents there are. Show them how many different kinds of fishing poles there are!*

Especially for Moms: *Plan a day when you have no plans when you get to the mall with the kids. Let THEM decide where to go, what to see, and what to eat at the mall. They will love it...and so will you. Promise...*

YOUNGER KIDS

SHOW them as many names of stores as you can. Read the names and have them point out letters and letter sounds that can be found in those store names. The mall is filled with letters and words. Use them!

ASK questions like, "Why can't we run in the mall?" "What would happen if we didn't pay for something at the store?" "What should kids do if they get lost from their Mom or Dad while they're at the mall?" "What does EXIT mean?" "What do you like best about the mall?" Their answers might surprise you!

TEACH them how to put things back on the shelves after they look at things in stores. Kids can learn to do it themselves, even when they are in a stroller!

OLDER KIDS

SHOW them the mall directory and see if they can show you where certain stores are. Stretch their thinking by asking them what the shortest route would be from one store to another or from the food court to a favorite store.

ASK them questions that will lead them to coming up with solutions to problems. For instance, you might say, "What do you think store managers should do if people don't pay for their food when they eat in restaurants?" "What should people do if they see kids stealing things from a store?" "What would you do if you saw a person choking on their food in the food court?" "What should the mall owners do if too many birds fly into the mall?"

TEACH them how to make good choices about things they want to buy at the mall. For instance, what do they need to look for when they try on sneakers or when they look for a school backpack? Lots of kids are influenced by what all the other kids have and they don't stop to think about what features THEY like and need.

MOVIE THEATER

Especially for Grandparents: Talk to Grandkids about how movie theaters have changed since you were their age. What were the screens like? How much did a ticket cost? How often did you go? What were the movies like? How much did popcorn and a coke cost then? Who did you go with? They can learn to appreciate what they have when they know what came before them. How will they know if we don't tell them?

YOUNGER KIDS

SHOW them where the EXIT signs are in movie theaters. Point to the sign and say, E-X-I-T…that tells us there is a door to go outside. See if they can find other EXIT signs. They will get good at finding them if you mention them every time you go.

ASK them questions that extend their thinking about the experience of going to a cinema. For instance, "What do people like to eat when they go to the movies?" "Why are there so many toilets and sinks in the bathroom?" "Where would you like to sit? Show me the seat."

TEACH them to hand the ticket to the ticket-taker and to say "thank you" when they are handed the stub. Tell them why they should save their ticket stub. They will enjoy doing this each time they go to the movies.

OLDER KIDS

SHOW them how to read the 'billboard' with movie titles and times. Tell them a movie title and see if they can find it and tell you what time it is playing that day. Tell them a time and see if they can find the movie that is playing then. This is good for visual scanning skills and for locating information quickly and easily.

ASK them about things that will tap into their imaginations. For instance, "How do you think they could make movie cinemas better?" "If you were the manager, what would you do to make sure people keep coming back to see movies there?" "How would you design a cinema so people could watch movies on the beach?" "What would a cinema look like if people wanted to watch a movie in booths with just their family and friends?"

TEACH them how to find and read movie reviews in the paper or on the internet. Why should they do this before they spend money on a movie? Do they know why?

NURSING HOME

"I guess we all wonder if we will still have something we can teach kids when we get old and gray. I remember when my next door neighbor asked me if I would watch her little 3-year-old girl while she worked a few mornings a week. I hadn't had any kids in my house for years and I wasn't sure what I would do with her! But, my dog Brenda and I figured we could handle one cute kid. She was cute, too....dark shiny hair and a million dollar smile. The Teachable Minute came when SHE taught ME how to change Barbie's clothes. She would say, "No, Mrs. C. Let me show you how to pull up her tights!!" And she did . . .
—Anne, Springfield, MA

Younger Kids

SHOW them some photos of older people and explain why some of them need to live in nursing homes. Help them understand that aging is a normal part of life and that it is important that we care for elderly people.

ASK questions that will help them understand what elderly people need. For example, "Do you think Grandma would like us to bring flowers or a book?" "Why do you think we need to visit people in a nursing home?" "Can you think of a picture to draw so we can hang it on the wall?" "What should we do if Grandma starts to cry?"

TEACH kids the importance of a smile and a hug. This will serve them well in life.

OLDER KIDS

SHOW them what a nursing home looks like so they understand what services are available for the elderly.

ASK them what they think they could do to cheer someone up who lives at a nursing home. Ask questions like, "What are some chores that elderly people have difficulty doing?" or "If you were a volunteer at a nursing home, what sorts of things could you do to help someone who is feeling bored?"

TEACH kids how to shake hands with someone. Elderly folks like when kids show respect by offering them a kind handshake. Many kids don't know the art of handshaking. It is a gesture of care, compassion, and friendliness.

PEDIATRICIAN'S OFFICE

Especially for Dads: *Kids love to examine people. Let them check your pulse while you teach them how many beats per minute is in the 'normal' range. Let them check your throat with a popsicle stick and your temperature with a thermometer. Oh, and kids love when Dads lay on the floor, closer to their level.*☺

Especially for Moms: *Think about letting kids pick out their favorite books or audio-tapes from home to take to the pediatrician's office. There is lots of waiting that goes on there. Picking out their favorite stories could make the time pass more quickly!*

YOUNGER KIDS

SHOW them words on index cards that are related to the doctor's office. If you can draw or glue on a picture to go with the word, that would be great. Have them point to each word with their 'pointer finger' as you read them aloud. Words you might use would be doctor, nurse, stethoscope, scale, thermometer, and Band-Aid©.

ASK questions that help them think about how they feel when they go to the doctor's office for a check-up. For instance, "Do you think kids like to go to the doctor?" "What do you like at the doctor's office?" "Why do you think some kids cry when they go to the doctor?" "Where do you want to go when we are all done at the doctor's office?"

TEACH them how to do a puzzle while at the doctor's office. Puzzles help increase attention span, reduce anxiety, and promote problem-solving skills.

OLDER KIDS

SHOW them how the scale at the doctor's office works. Lots of kids are curious about it, but they never get a chance to see how their weight is measured.

ASK them questions like, "Why do you think people become doctors?" "What's the best thing about being a doctor and what's the worst thing?" "Why are there so many different kinds of doctors?" "Why do you think lots of people are afraid to go to the doctor?"

TEACH them how to deal with the common cold. What are some things they can do to alleviate the symptoms? What are some medicines, foods, and drinks they should have when they have a cold? Discuss some of the possible reasons why we get colds and what can be done to reduce them.

PET SHOP

<small>◇◇◇◇◇◇◇◇◇◇◇◇◇◇◇◇◇◇◇</small>

Especially for Grandparents: Share your stories about the pets that have been a part of your life or of the lives of people you know. What were their names and why were they special? What do you want kids to know about caring for a pet? Teach them the oldie, but goodie song, "How Much is That Doggie in the Window?"

YOUNGER KIDS

SHOW them pictures of pets and have them name them. Encourage them to use descriptive words to go with the type of animal it is. For example, show them a photo or picture of a big cat and say, "Big fluffy cat" or show them a white dog and say, "Little white dog." Remember to include fish, hamsters, guinea pigs, lizards, hermit crabs, rabbits, and any other pet you can think of!

ASK questions while you are in the pet shop that will help them learn what supplies pets need. "Can you show me the doggie's leash? Point and show me." "Can you show me the kitty's bowl? Point and show me." "Can you show me the hamster's cage? Point and show me." "Can you show me the aquarium? Point and show me."

TEACH them about pet toys while you are there. Point out how toys for cats are different from toys for dogs, and why.

OLDER KIDS

SHOW them different kinds of fish there are at a pet store. There are so many! Point out all the supplies that are needed to keep fish healthy in an aquarium.

ASK kids questions that will lead to a greater understanding of how to care for pets. For instance, you might say, "What would we to buy if we were going to get a hamster?" "Why do you think there are so many different kinds of dog food?" "What do you think is the best kind of bed for a dog or cat?" "Why do you think there are so many different kinds of dog bones?"

TEACH them how to read the labels on pet products. Are there any instructions that are provided? Kids tend to 'skip' the instructions on most labels…a funny phenomenon! ☺

POLICE STATION

"My kids were always afraid of the police. We lived in the upper west side of New York City and they grew up hearing lots of sirens through the day and night. We had two dogs that the kids would take for walks to Central Park every day after school. One day, our chocolate lab saw another dog and bolted. Our son started screaming when the leash flew out of his hand and 'Brownie' was gone. He saw a police officer and asked him if he could find his dog. He told me that the policeman used his walkie-talkie and then told him to sit on the park bench and "not move." He did as he was told and twenty minutes later, our son saw the policeman walking towards him with Brownie. That night, he wrote a letter to the policeman and included a picture of Brownie. He was never afraid of the police again. He says he still remembers that the most important thing the officer told him was to "not move" on the park bench. Now THAT was a TEACHABLE MINUTE for my son. Thanks, Officer. "

—Ryan, Albany, NY

YOUNGER KIDS

SHOW them a book about police officers. Expose them to new words like badge, police car, siren, boots, police dog, ticket, and flashing lights. Kids are curious about the police!

ASK questions that will help them label what they see at the station. "Where is the police car?" "Where is the policeman's hat?" "Where is the policeman's badge?" "Where is the police dog?" Police station employees love to show kids around. What else would they help your kids notice?

TEACH them how to ask for help. Say things like, "If somebody took our car, we would call the police and tell them where we were and what our car looks like," or "If we saw a stranger following us home from the bus stop, we would call the police and tell them what street we are on so they could come and check it out." It's not too early to teach kids how to ask for help. Practice with them.

OLDER KIDS

SHOW them a book or a video about the duties and responsibilities that police officers have. Many kids don't realize that police officers also serve at sporting events, concerts, movies, racetracks, amusement parks, museums, hospitals, and construction sites.

ASK them questions like, "How do you think the radio dispatcher keeps track of all the calls that come into the station?" "How is a police car different than our car?" "What are police dogs trained to do?" "How do you think police stations are similar to fire stations?" You may want to ask a police officer some of these questions while you are at the station.

TEACH kids how to respect authority without being afraid of it. Teach them that it is perfectly acceptable to ask a police officer to see his or her badge if they are at all unsure about whether someone really is an officer or not.

PARK BENCH

Especially for Dads: *How does someone build a park bench? Show kids how sometimes a simple design can be the best design.*
Especially for Moms: *Teach kids how to watch pets and people go by while they sit on a bench. Model that for them and maybe talk about what you learn when you watch the world go by. Ahhhh...*

YOUNGER KIDS

SHOW them all the things they can see from a park bench. Name them. For example, a sidewalk, trees, leaves, bark, a nest, a pond, a girl, a boy, adults, a stroller, grass, dirt, swings, a playground, clouds, and the sky!

ASK them questions such as "What does the dog say?" If they don't say, "Bow Wow or Woof Woof," then you say it and invite them to copy you. Do the same for the following: "What does the pig say?" "What does the cow say?" "What does the cat say?" "What does the lion say?" "What does the horse say?"

TEACH them how to count to 100. A park bench is a great place to count!

OLDER KIDS

SHOW kids how to play Tic-Tac-Toe or Hangman while you are sitting on a park bench together. These simple games require them to think in new and different ways.

ASK questions that help kids draw conclusions. For instance, "Why do you think that dog won't drop the ball no matter what his owner says or does to get him to drop the ball?" "How old do you think that tree is?" "Why do you think they took down the wooden playground?" "How do you think the park rangers know when it's safe to ice skate on the pond in the winter?" "Why do you think that kid is laughing/crying/shouting/running?"

TEACH kids the value of sitting quietly for a minute, or two. A park bench is a great place to relax and 'be still.'

PARKING GARAGE

"Almost every day, my daughter would ask me if we could go to the parking garage. We had been to one a few times when we took my husband to the airport and when we went to the mall. I couldn't figure out why she wanted to go so much. When I asked her, she just said, "Because I want to, Mom." The next time we went to a parking garage, my daughter said, "Oh good. Now our car can sleep." I finally figured out why she came to that conclusion. We lived in an apartment and didn't have a garage. Our car was always parked out on the street. I guess she thought it couldn't "sleep" there!"

—Elaine, Chicago, IL

YOUNGER KIDS

SHOW kids how fun it is to drive to the top floor of the parking garage. Often, this floor is outdoors. You can count the floors together as you go up. Go all the way to the top! When you get out of the car, what can you show them?

ASK them to find different colored cars as you walk through the parking garage or on your way to the elevator. "Can you find a blue car? There it is." "Can you find a red car? There it is." "Can you find a black car? There it is." "Can you find a car that looks like our car? There is one."

TEACH them how to count cars or license plates as you pass by them.

OLDER KIDS

SHOW them how to park the car in a parking space. Talk through it as you do it. It's not as easy as it may seem!

ASK questions that will help kids think about what it takes to design a parking garage. For instance, "How do you think they know how wide to make the spaces for cars to park in?" "Are all the spaces the same length and width?" "Why do you think trucks are not allowed to park in parking garages?" "How do you think they painted the lines on the garage floor for the car spaces?" "Why are there so many exit signs?" "How do people remember which floor and space they parked in?" "Why do we have to pay for parking our car in a parking garage?"

TEACH them how to calculate how much it will cost to park in that garage for different amounts of time. For instance, if it costs $2.00 per hour, ask them what it will cost if they stay there for 3 and 1/2 hours? 6 hours? 24 hours?

RESTROOM

Especially for Dads: *So…what do boys need to know about the men's rest room, Dad? How about telling them how water magically appears when we turn on the sink faucet…and where it goes when it goes down the drain?*

Especially for Moms: *How about a talk about what to do if there is no toilet paper left or if the stall door won't open or if the toilet seat is all wet? Good things to know, Mom!*

YOUNGER KIDS

SHOW them how special they are when you hold them up to a mirror. Say, "I like myself" when you hold a baby or toddler up to a mirror. Say it several times, and often. If you are with a young child say something like, "Look how shiny your hair looks" or "Wow, your teeth look so white when you smile" or "I like the way you smile."

ASK some silly questions like "Do you see puppies in here?" "Do you see bunny rabbits in here?" "Do you see elephants in here?" "Do you see tigers in here?" "Do you see balloons in here?" "Do you see clowns in here?" "Do you see cars in here?" Kids love silly questions!

TEACH kids how to point and say the names of everything they see in the restroom: toilet, wall, light, ceiling, door, door handle, toilet paper, sink, paper towel, dryer, mirror, faucet, trash can, and whatever word or picture is on the door to identify whether it's for MEN or WOMEN.

OLDER KIDS

SHOW them how to wash their hands properly. Believe it or not, there are many kids who don't know how or why they need to know how to do that well!

ASK open-ended questions while you're in the restroom. An open-ended question cannot be answered with a 'yes' or a 'no' response. For instance, "What would you like to do this weekend?" "How would you like to celebrate your birthday this year?" "What is the most annoying thing that happens when you're on the school bus?" Try to limit the number of 'yes' and 'no' questions you ask and see what happens to your conversations with kids.

TEACH them what to do and say if a stranger approaches them at a public place. Tell them what you would do. Encourage them to trust their instincts when something doesn't 'feel' right to them.

"I have twin 6-year-old boys. When they were around 4, we spend a lot of time with beginning sounds in words. One night, one of the boys called me into his room. He was giggling away and then he asked, "Mom, what letter does POOP start with?!" I helped him figure it out. He kept giggling and I knew he was learning to match sounds with letters!"

—Amber, Hartford, CT

REST STOP

"I guess you could say my husband and I found out the meaning of the teachable minute when we pulled into a highway rest stop to get gas and clean the windshield. When we were ready to go our youngest said, "Mom and Dad, why is it called a rest stop if we never rest and stop?" HE was catching the teachable minute so we would learn something too. Kids are teachers, too!"

—Mark & Cindy-San Diego, CA

YOUNGER KIDS

SHOW them books about cars, trucks, planes, buses, rockets, and trains while you're at a rest stop. Books teach!

ASK questions like, "What can fly?" "What can carry heavy things?" "What can go on a track?" "What can take kids to school?" "What can take us to the moon?" "What are we sitting in right now?" If they don't know, tell them. Then start again. Repetition is also a good teacher.

TEACH younger kids how to stop, look, and walk in a busy parking lot. Don't rely on taking their hand and pulling them along. Even if they can't talk yet, you can still say, "Stop. Look. Walk." They will learn what those mean, soon.

OLDER KIDS

SHOW kids where you are on a paper or GPS map. Ask them to identify things that are nearby such as a city, highway, ocean, or mountain. Mapping skills are so important.

ASK questions that will help kids analyze information. Examples of these would be, "What's the cost of regular unleaded gas and super gas? Why is 'super' more?" "Why do fast food places have 'combo' meals? Is it better to buy a combo meal or not?" "Why do you think stores have items 'on sale'?"

TEACH kids how to find states on a U.S. map or a city on a WORLD map. Keep at it until they can do this quickly and easily. It may take a few rest stops!

RESTAURANT

❖❖❖❖❖❖❖❖❖❖❖❖❖❖❖❖❖❖❖❖❖❖

Especially for Grandparents: What do you think kids would like to know about while they're waiting for their food to arrive? How about what restaurants looked like when you were a child? Were there fast food restaurants? Where there drive-up windows? How much did an ice cream cone cost? Was there a kids' menu? Kids can learn to appreciate what they have if they hear how far things have progressed.

YOUNGER KIDS

SHOW them all the pictures on a menu or a placemat. Point to each one and say what it is. See if they can copy you.

ASK kids food questions such as "Is a donut a vegetable?" "Is milk green?" "Is ice cream hot?" "Is a banana orange?" "Is a cookie a fruit?" "Are eggs purple?" "Are pumpkins orange?" "Are oranges orange?" "Are apples square or round?" "Can we eat rocks?!" Remember, young kids like it when we get silly!☺

TEACH kids how to count sugar packets, spoons, straws, and anything else on the table that can be counted. Write the numbers 0 – 10 on a napkin or on the back of a placemat and teach them how to point and say them, forwards and backwards.

114

OLDER KIDS

SHOW them how a menu is organized and where they can find certain types of foods quickly and easily. A menu can be a good teacher.

ASK questions that keep kids' minds busy while they are waiting in a restaurant. Examples might be, "How much would it cost if we each got four burgers and two milkshakes?" "What's the most expensive thing on the menu?" "What do you think if the most popular food on the menu?" "How do you think restaurant owners decide how much to charge for each item?" Keep those minds busy until the food arrives. Then let them eat!

TEACH kids how to speak clearly when they order what they would like to eat. Too many kids 'slur' their words and they can't be understood. No matter what language is spoken, diction and pronunciation is important. In fact, did you know that the best spellers in the world have the best diction? When we speak clearly, we can hear the sounds in words. Diction matters!

"I am a Grandmother of twin boys. When they were 4 years old they came over for lunch. They thought my kitchen was a restaurant! As I pulled out two boiled ears of corn from a big pot on the stove, one of them asked, "What is that Yiayia (Grandma)?" I told them it was corn on the cob and grown on a farm. "Oh no," said Grandson Tom, "Corn comes from a bag in the freezer, Yiayia!" You can't imagine the fun I had teaching them how to spread butter on it, hold the ends, and bite into it. They loved eating it like that!"

—Yiayia, Amherst, MA

115

SHOE STORE

"Sam was working hard on becoming a good reader. He knew that he did not read as well as his friends did and he was determined to change that. He took his books home every night and was so happy each time I gave him higher level books. He would keep track of the numbers on the front of his little books. He could read level 3's, 4's, 5's, and 6's by December. Then one morning, Sam came running into the classroom and said, "Look, Mrs. Reynolds. My Mom took me shopping for sneakers. I'm on level 10's!!" I decided to let Sam think that his shoe size was the same as his reading levels. He was reading way past 'level 10' in just a few short weeks and I'm sure his feet grew just as quickly!"
—Mrs. Reynolds, Grade 1, Columbus, OH

YOUNGER KIDS

SHOW them all the different kinds of shoes in a shoe store. As you hold up each shoe, tell them its color. Then point to a shoe and see if they can tell you its color. They will catch on quickly.

ASK questions that will help kids identify the sounds, 'sh,' 'ch,' 'th', 'wh' at the beginning of words. "What sound does SHOE start with?" "What sound does SHAMPOO start with?" "What sound does CHICKEN start with?" "What sound does THAT start with?" "What sound does WHITE start with? Tell them other words that start like these words do.

TEACH them how to put shoes back in a shoe box with the cover on, too. It may sound simple, but kids will find it a challenge. Let them practice with different types of shoes.

OLDER KIDS

SHOW them how to look for their size shoe on the side of shoe boxes. What else does the label on the shoe box tell them? Can they also find their shoe size written on the shoe somewhere? Are both shoes the same size? How do they know that?

ASK questions that will encourage them to do some research to find the answers. "When did someone invent sneakers?" "Why were they called 'sneakers'?" "What material is used to make sneakers?" "How many companies sell sneakers?" "About how much did sneakers cost 20 years ago and what do they cost now?" "Why do people like sneakers?" You can ask the same types of questions with any kind of shoes such as leather shoes, boots, dress shoes, ballet shoes, bowling shoes, construction books, etc.

TEACH them how to tell if a shoe fits them well or not. Kids often pick out shoes that look like shoes their friends are wearing, regardless of how they feel! Discuss the importance of comfort and durability. Show them how to check—squeeze the heel of a sneaker to be sure that it's good and strong. If not, it won't last long.

SIDEWALK

Especially for Dads: *How are sidewalks made? Show kids a book or video about cement mixers. Kids would soak that stuff up!*
Especially for Moms: *Teach kids how to 'window shop.' It's a great way to point out lots of things that kids might not notice unless you stop and look. It will be fun for you, too!*

YOUNGER KIDS

SHOW them how to hop (on two feet and then on one foot). Then show them how to skip, gallop, and tiptoe on a sidewalk. Sidewalks aren't just for walking, you know!

ASK questions that help kids think about the world around them as you take a walk or a stroll on a sidewalk. For example, ask them to point to things as you say, "Where is the house? There it is." "Where is the fence? There it is" "Where is the flag? There it is." "Where is the playground? There it is." "Where is the mailbox? There it is." "Where is the bus? There it is." "Where is the bicycle? There it is!" If they don't know, point with them as you say, "There it is." They will catch on if you do this enough.

TEACH them how to count and walk. Can they count by ones, twos, and fives as they walk with you? Walk slowly and count together. Walk quickly and count together. Walk backwards and count together. Walk and count!

OLDER KIDS

SHOW them how to obey traffic light signals when crossing streets. Do they know what a crosswalk is and why they need to cross within the lines?

ASK them questions about front yards or store fronts. For instance, "How do sidewalks help store owners?" "Why do people put fences up in their front lawns?" "If you had a store or a restaurant, what could you do to get people to come into your store?" "Why do you think some people's mailboxes down at the bottom of their driveway near the sidewalk or street?"

TEACH kids how to walk on the right side of a sidewalk. Many kids don't know this!

VET'S OFFICE

"What can a pet teach a child? A lot! Our black lab got a ball stuck deep in his throat when we were playing catch. The more we tried to get it out, the deeper it went into his throat. I was beside myself and thought he was going to die in our arms. I held him in my arms in the car. Dad sped to the nearest vet. My dog was barely breathing and I was sick with fear that he might not make it. Fortunately, the vet was working overtime and was just locking up when we pulled up. He put him to sleep and took the ball out. In 30 minutes, we were at home and my dog was licking my face and looking for food! My teachable minute came when I saw how my dog did not panic when he was hurt. He was brave, stoic, and calm even when he could barely breathe. I will remember that if I am ever hurt. He's gone now, but I learned so many things from my dog. He was a great teacher."

—Gabriel, Boston, MA

YOUNGER KIDS

SHOW kids how to keep a pet calm while at the vet. We do this by using our voices in a low, slow, reassuring way. We also can calm a pet with a loving touch. Kids need to know this.

ASK kids questions that will teach 'feeling' words. "Is that puppy feeling sad?" "How do you know?" "Is our dog feeling scared?" "Is the cat feeling frightened?" "Is that dog feeling happy?"

TEACH them how to play 'Mother (or Father) May I?' while you're waiting to see the vet. It's a timeless game that teaches kids how to follow oral directions. They stand about 10 feet, or more, away from you. You say, "You may take 5 baby steps forward." They ask, "Mother may I?" You either say "Yes, you may" or "No, you may not." If they forget to ask, "Mother may I?" they have to go back to the start. Whoever tags you first, is the winner! Fun game that teaches much!

OLDER KIDS

SHOW them a book or video about different breeds of dogs or cats. There are many! See if they can find features that are similar and different.

ASK questions that help kids understand the role of a veterinarian. For instance, "Why do you think someone would want to become a veterinarian?" "Do you think it's as hard as being a human doctor?" "Why do you think that?" "What are some of the things a vet has to know?" "What do you think the hardest part of the job is?"

TEACH them how to describe symptoms to the vet. Role-play the visit before you go or while you're in the car on the way. What do you think the vet needs to know? Why is it important for us to tell the vet everything we can about our pet's condition? Kids don't naturally know what to say to doctors. They need help with this!

RECREATIONAL SPOTS

If kids could play all day, they would!

ENCOURAGE PLAY…

For more information on how to
ENCOURAGE PLAY with your kids visit:
theteachableminute.com/encourage

AMUSEMENT PARK

"When Bert and I took Michael and Jane on the merry-go-round, we never dreamed they would have their mouths wide open the entire time. A fly or some sort of nasty bug could have flown in and out of their mouths several times if I did not watch them very closely. I think what shocked them the most was when the horses galloped right out into the pasture. Well, I dare say I just don't know why that would surprise them so. Isn't that what horses should do? They don't just go 'up and down,' you know…they must run! Oh well, my teachable minute came when later that evening, I sang the children a song about why they should NOT go to sleep. Funny, but they did!"

—Mary Poppins, England

YOUNGER KIDS

SHOW kids a map of the amusement park when you first arrive. Point and say where things are so they know what the names of the rides are.

ASK kids about what kinds of things they would like to do at the amusement park. For example, you might ask, "Do you want to ride on the merry-go-round or the bumper cars?" "Do you want to go on a slide or a swing ride?" "Do you want to watch the big kids go on a roller coaster or watch them ride on flying saucers?" "Do you want to throw balls or do sand art?" Even if they don't talk yet, it is still good to give them choices and let them hear what questions sound like.

TEACH them how to use signs find things in an amusement park. Show them the exit signs, restroom signs, gift shop signs, ride signs, and any other sign you can find. Point out letters on the signs or whole words they might know such as 'walk,' 'no,' 'stop,' 'in,' 'out.'

OLDER KIDS

SHOW kids the place where they should go if they get separated from you. See if they can find it on the park map and mark it with a big circle. Be sure they keep a map with them all day in case they need it.

ASK questions that will help them prioritize their choices for what they would like to do. You may want to help by breaking it down into morning and afternoon. For instance, "What do you think would be a good route before lunch? Show me on the map. Can you find where we are now?" "Where should we eat lunch? See if you can find the symbol for 'food' on the map. Which one looks best?" "What should we plan to do after lunch?"

TEACH kids how to enjoy each ride they are on. Lots of kids are so busy thinking about which ride they will go on next that they don't stop to think about the one they are on. You can do this by asking them what they liked (or didn't like) about the ride they just came off of or to describe, in one word, what they ride was like.

BASEBALL GAME

"There is just no better place to catch the teachable minute than at a ball game, if you want the truth. Kids can learn anything here. When I took my 2 sons to a game, I taught them how to count the bases, keep track of the balls and strikes, cheer the team on, and eat a hotdog in record time. What else do they need to know?!"

—Leonard, Milwaukee, WI

YOUNGER KIDS

SHOW kids all the things they can do with a ball. Can they throw it to you? Can they roll it on the floor and catch it when it comes rolling back to them? Can they throw it up in the air and across the yard? A ball can do lots of things!

ASK them questions about what they see at a baseball game. For instance, "Do you see baseball players? Clap your hands!" "Do you see the baseball? Clap your hands!" "Do you see the score board? Clap your hands!" "Do you see some lots of people? Clap your hands!" Clapping is fun…

TEACH them how to draw easy things that are part of the game of baseball such as a ball, a bat, a baseball glove, a baseball hat, and a baseball diamond. They copy you or make up their own.

OLDER KIDS

SHOW them how to understand the score board at a baseball game. Do they know what a ball and a strike is? Do they know what the term 'bases loaded' means? Do they know what it means when someone 'steals' a base? Build their vocabulary and concept development.

ASK kids things that will teach them about being a good team player. For instance, "What do you think you should say to someone on your team if they strike out?" "What could say to a friend who wants to quit the team?" "What is the best thing to do if someone on the team starts a fight with you?" "What do you think a coach should say to kids to help them play well?"

TEACH them how to be a good sport, whether their team wins or loses. What matters most? Do they know? This will help them in many areas of life, not just when they go to a game.

BASKETBALL GAME

Especially for Dads: *What does it take to dribble a ball well? Teach kids how to dribble. You will be helping their eye-hand coordination as well as their coordination. Dribble away!*

Especially for Moms: *Get a 'squishy' basketball and a small kids' hoop that attaches to the refrigerator. When the kids are fussy or bored, take the ball and shout, "She jumps, she shoots, SCORE!" They will want more. Try using a plastic cup, a measuring cup, a plastic spoon, a lollipop, and anything else that you can 'jump and shoot' with. What a FUN MOM!*

YOUNGER KIDS

SHOW them a book about basketball so they know what it's about. When you go to a game, point and say the names of things that you see, such as COURT, HOOP, REFEREE, PLAYERS, COACH, CHEERLEADERS, BASKETBALL, SCORE BOARD, and POPCORN!

ASK them if they can clap and say words such as, "Can you clap and say 'snowball'?" "Can you clap and say 'baseball'?" "Can you clap and say 'volleyball'?" "Can you clap and say, "basketball'? If they can't do it yet, take their hands in yours and 'clap and say' each word together!

TEACH them how to 'jump and shoot.' If you don't have a hoop, they can easily 'jump and shoot' the ball at a wall or the side of the garage. Jump and shoot for exercise!

OLDER KIDS

SHOW them some famous basketball players in a book or on a video. Talk about what it takes to be a great basketball player.

ASK questions during the game that will help them engage with what is going on. For instance, you might ask, "Why doesn't everybody get a chance to shoot the ball?" "What does double-dribble mean?" "Does blocking really work?" Kids love to explain things to adults. Listen attentively and they will tell you everything you need to know!

TEACH them how to use binoculars during the game. If you don't have one, give them two plastic cups with the bottoms cut out of them. See if they can follow the game better. Cool!

BEACH

◇◇◇◇◇◇◇◇◇◇◇◇◇

Especially for Grandparents: Start kids on a collection of seashells. You can find them together, wash them together, and sort them according to size or shape. Kids will learn to value things that are part of a collection, as you probably know. While you're looking for shells together, you may want to teach them the song, "By the sea, by the sea, by the beautiful sea…" or any song. The beach is a perfect place to sing!

YOUNGER KIDS

SHOW kids how to make a mud pie. Bring a small pie plate or cereal bowl from home so their creation really looks like a pie. What does beach sand and water make? Mud!

ASK questions about who lives in the sea by bringing a book or two about 'sea life' with you when you go to the beach. For instance, hold up the picture of a dolphin and say, "What is this?" Do the same for other creatures such as a whale, shark, seahorse, starfish, and octopus. If they don't know, tell them. Then go back and try it again later in the day.

TEACH creativity at the beach. What can you build out of sand together? Remember that the beach is one giant sandbox!

OLDER KIDS

SHOW them how to write postcards to friends and relatives. Let them choose the postcards they like and then encourage them to share what they are seeing and doing at the beach. Postcards are short and simple to do which is exactly why we want to engage kids in doing them. What they can write, they can read. Write, Write, and Write…postcards help with that.

ASK questions that will get kids to explore all the different things that people do on and near the ocean. For example, "Why do you think surfboards are shaped the way they are?" "How do people stay on top of the water when they water ski?" "Why is a kayak easier to paddle than a canoe?" "What's the difference between scuba diving and snorkeling?" Even if they don't know the answers, you will have food for thought…and hopefully, future exploration.

TEACH kids how to play checkers or chess on the beach. They will learn how many things including patience, strategizing, sportsmanship, and perseverance. These are TIMELESS games. Use them!

BOWLING ALLEY

"I always took the kids bowling during their school vacations. It was fun and they loved it. I remember when my youngest found the teachable minute when he was only 3 years old! He didn't want to bowl that day so he sat on the bench as watched us all bowl. I asked him if he wanted to try it and he would say, "Not yet, Mom." When we were almost done, he announced that he was ready for his turn. We all tried to help him since he had never done it before, but he refused to let us help him. He said, "I know how." He picked up the ball with two hands and slowly walked up to the line. He spread his legs and bent over, holding his ball with both hands, way down low. Then he slowly swung the ball backwards then forwards (between his legs) and dropped it. It moved very slowly down the middle of the lane and then, WHAM!! His ball knocked every single pin down instantly. Everyone started screaming and cheering for him. He turned and said, "See…I told you I knew how!" The amazing thing is that he did it several more times with the same results! I guess he taught us!"

—Lori, Seattle, Washington

YOUNGER KIDS

SHOW them how to roll ball on the floor at home so they will know how when they get to the bowling alley. A hallway can serve as a great bowling alley, using balls made out of plastic or foam. Can they knock an empty milk carton down at the end of the hallway?

ASK the 'yes and no' questions that about what they see in the bowling alley. For example, "Do you see a boy with a blue shirt?"

"Do you see your brother?" "Do you see a snowman?" "Do you see a bowling ball?" "Do you see a bunny rabbit?" If they can't say "yes" and "no" yet, teach them to shake their head with the correct response. They will catch on if you do this often, in different places.

TEACH them how to write the letter 'O' on paper, on a whiteboard, or on the bowling alley score pad. Show them the shape of the ball. Hold their hand and trace the letter 'O" in the air with them. Then write the letter 'O' with them. Then let them try to write it on their OWN!

OLDER KIDS

SHOW them how to the game of bowling is played. You may want to watch a video on the internet or read a book about it together before you go. What's the object of the game?

ASK questions that will help them think about how to improve their bowling skills. "How do you think people keep the ball from going in the gutter?" "Does it matter how your fingers are placed in the hole?" "Is it easier for you to use a lighter bowling ball?" "What does your wrist have to do with the way the ball goes?" "Do you find it easier to take two steps or three steps when you get ready to throw the ball?"

TEACH kids how to compliment you and anyone else they are with. Kids don't think that adults need feedback. Show them how and they will become adults who support other adults in good ways.

CAMPGROUND

Especially for Dads: *If you think your kids are spending too much time in front of screens, consider a few camping experiences with them, even you have to camp out in the back yard or on the deck! Let them help you make a list of supplies that will be needed along with a list of chores that must be done to get everything set up. Teach survival!*

Especially for Moms: *Read descriptions of what different campgrounds offer in your state or around the country. Ask kids which ones they think would be better than others and why. Not all campgrounds are alike!*

YOUNGER KIDS

SHOW them how to make a tent out of a big sheet or blanket. You can drape it over a small table or over two back-to-back chairs so they can crawl under it. Put some books in there about camping or about tents. Fun!

ASK kids questions that help reinforce beginning sounds, using words that go with 'camping.' For instance, "What sound does TENT start with?" "What sound does TREE start with?" "What sound does RAIN start with?" "What sound does FOREST start with?" "What sound does LAKE start with?" "What sound does CAMPER start with?" "What sound does MARSHMALLOW start with?

TEACH kids a camp song or tell them a story about their favorite stuffed animal who decided to go camping. They love to hear stories about their own toys. Make them up…they will beg for more!

OLDER KIDS

SHOW them a website or a catalog displaying all kinds of tents and campers. Help them look for information below each photo. Show them how to look for reviews from customers and have them pick their favorite ones.

ASK questions that will help kids think about outdoor survival skills and safety. For example, "What should people do to make sure they don't start a fire in the woods?" "What will we do if start to see lots of ants and other bugs crawling around our tent or camper?" "What should we do if we see a skunk at our campsite?" "What's the most important drink we should have plenty of?"

TEACH kids how to fold sheets and towels. Encourage them to help set up a clothesline with some strong rope.

FOOTBALL GAME

"One day I asked my son to give his little sister a banana for her snack. I heard him go into the kitchen and then he told her to go out for a pass! I peeked into the kitchen and saw her running into the living room with her ponytail bobbing up and down. She stood by the fireplace with her hands in front of her. I couldn't believe what I was seeing! The he shouted, "Look up," as he threw the banana towards her like it was a football. She didn't even blink. She just reached up, caught the banana, and ran back into the kitchen. He screamed, "Touchdown!!" She peeled the banana, sat down on the floor, and ate it. I guess my son caught a 'teachable minute' with his sister, and I really couldn't argue with that!"

—Martha, Cheyenne, WY

YOUNGER KIDS

SHOW them small paper footballs that you taped to things all over the kitchen. On each football should be the name of the object that the football is taped to. Be sure to write each word in lower-case letters. Go over to each football together and say, "Let's point and read."

ASK kids questions that will help kids know what is happening at a football game, whether it's live or on television. For example, "Where is the sky?" "Where is the football?" "Where are the football players?" "Where is the football field?" Where is the big net?" Where are the bleachers?" For little ones, you will still want to ask and then point with them.

TEACH them how to throw and catch a soft football (not a banana!). It is different from throwing and catching a baseball or basketball.

Older Kids

SHOW them a book about football so they can understand how the game is played. Too many kids go on to middle school and high school without really knowing what this game is about!

ASK questions that will lead them to drawing conclusions such as, "If a player keeps dropping the ball, what do you think the coach will do?" "When the quarterback throws the ball, how does he know who to throw it to?" "What do you think a coin toss if for?" "Why does a referee throw a red flag on the field?" "Why do football players wear shoes that have cleats on the bottom of them?"

TEACH them how to look up words like game, stadium, sport, score, regulations, coach, and player in a thesaurus. What other words can they find that mean similar things? This will build their vocabulary while also teaching them important words that are linked to the game of football.

MINIATURE GOLF

Especially for Dads: *Kids might like to know how 'real golf' is the same, and different, from 'miniature golf.'*

Especially for Moms: *Got a long wooden spoon and a small plastic ball for kids to practice playing golf at home? You can also use a long empty wrapping paper roll to serve as a golf club. Kids actually like using these 'everyday items' better than they do the plastic indoor golf clubs! Try it and see...*

YOUNGER KIDS

SHOW them a brochure or website about miniature golf before you go. Point out the names of things they will need to know such as golf club, ball, hole, green, bridge, kids, and water. Most miniature golf places have all of these things.

ASK questions like, "Where will we start playing? Yes, Hole #1." "Where will we go after that?" "Then where?" Keep going until you get to #18. While you're playing, stop and ask, "Which hole are we on?" If they can't remember, take them back to the sign to point and say the number. Teach signs!

TEACH them how to use their golf club to measure things. For instance, hold the golf club next to them to see how high it comes up to on them. Then have them measure other things by the length of the golf club. Some examples might be your arm, the height of the stroller, a bush, or a bench.

OLDER KIDS

SHOW kids how to use the golf course score card. Lots of kids don't like to use it because they don't understand what 'par' means. Straighten that out so they can do some math while they are keeping track of golf scores.

ASK them to think about their strategy when they are playing. Some examples of questions would be, "Why do you think golfers lay down their clubs between their ball and the hole when they get close to getting it in?" "Why do you think some people hit a side wall on purpose?" "How can you keep your ball from sliding over the hole so you can get it into the hole?" "Is it easier for you to go first or last?" Let them 'own' their game!

TEACH fair play. Some kids try to move their ball or make excuses why one of their hits didn't count. If kids are taught how to play by the rules from the beginning, they will know what is expected.

MUSEUM

◇◇◇◇◇◇◇◇◇◇◇◇◇◇◇◇◇◇◇◇

I took the kids to our local museum every school vacation for about ten years. Do you know what they remember about it? They remember the stuffed bunny that was in a glass case with lights on him. When the lights changed color, so did he! I wish they remembered more than just the bunny, but I did use him to teach them about the concept of 'camouflage.'

—Betty, Council Bluff, IA

YOUNGER KIDS

SHOW kids what things are in a museum without boring them. Too many kids get turned off to museums from a young age because the tour is too slow. Today's kids have adapted to a faster pace because of the influences of television and technology. They will get just as much out of it if you move the tour along. The goal is to have them WANT to go, again and again!

ASK questions that help them find things as you are touring the museum. For instance, "Where do you see a brown owl? Show me!" "Where do you see a map? Show me!" "Where do you see something that is bigger than you are? Show me!" "Where do you see something that is red? Show me?" "Where do you see a painting on the wall? Show me!"

TEACH respect. When kids understand that a museum is a place to learn about old and interesting things, they appreciate it more. They will come to know that this is not a place to play.

OLDER KIDS

SHOW them a book or website with the most famous museums in the world. How many people visit them each year? What city and country are they located in? Which ones would they like to go to some day?

ASK questions such as, "Why do you think there are alarms in museums?" "How do people find things to go into a museum?" "If you wanted to work in a museum, what job would you like best?" "How do you think they clean large things that hang from the ceilings?" "If you could own a museum, what would you put in it? Would it be one kind of thing or lots of different things?"

TEACH them how to read the museum map. If they were going to design their own museum, would they use the same layout? What would they keep the same and what would they change?

SWIMMING POOL

Especially for Dads: *Take kids to a pool store or watch a video together about how pools are placed above and below the ground. Kids are curious! They swim in them, but they don't know how they were built.*

Especially for Moms: *While you're in the car with the kids, consider telling them stories that will teach them pool safety rules such as not diving in shallow water, running next to the pool, shouting "help" when help is not needed, or jumping in when a lot of kids are in the water. Kids remember lessons well when they are woven into STORIES. They will beg you to tell those stories over and over again. True!*

YOUNGER KIDS

SHOW them pictures or books about kids who are swimming. Talk about what is happening in the pictures. Talk, Talk, Talk! They will listen…and learn.

ASK action questions that will help kids learn different movements in the pool. Say, "Can you splash the water with your hands? Let me see." "Can you splash the water with your legs? "Can you hold onto the wall and kick?" "Can you climb up the pool steps all by yourself? "

TEACH them how to watch other kids so they will learn new things. Encourage this by saying, "What are those kids doing? Let's sit and watch them." We all learn from watching others do things well.

OLDER KIDS

SHOW kids different swim strokes so they can find the one they like best of all. You might find a video that shows people swimming the breast stroke, back stroke, butterfly stroke, and side stroke. These strokes are hard for some kids to learn. Let them choose which ones they would like to work on.

ASK them if they would like you to 'rate' them as they jump into the deep end of the pool in different ways. For instance, say "Ok. Jump in with both legs straight and arms by your side." When they surface, hold up the number of fingers they scored on that jump (10 fingers being the highest and 1 finger being the lowest). Suggest other jumps such as both arms wrapped around your right knee, arms out to the side and legs spread wide, or arms up high and legs crossed at the ankles. They love the rating system and they will do these jumps over and over until they see 10 fingers!

TEACH kids how to keep a ball up in the air while you're in the pool together. See how many times you can pass it back and forth without the ball touching the water. Fun . . .

ZOO

◇◇◇◇◇◇◇◇◇

My Granddaughter has always loved horses. Her Mom use to ride horses before she died and now she does, too. When she was 12 years old, I took her to a zoo that also had several pastures. As we passed one of the pastures, she noticed a brown horse, standing very far from us. She said, "Grandma, do you have one of those apples we brought?" I handed her the apple and she stood by the fence with her arm outstretched and the apple in her palm. She whistled and called out softly to the horse a few times, but he didn't budge. After about 15 minutes, I told her I was going to go over to a bench and sit down. I watched her stand there, for 45 minutes, until that horse finally came over to her, took the apple in his mouth, and let her pet him. Her patience was remarkable and I'll never forget that. She named him, "Noble."

—Elizabeth, Williamsburg, VA

YOUNGER KIDS

SHOW them pictures of zoo animals. Then tell them a silly thing about one of the animals in a complete sentence. For instance, "That monkey likes lollipops!" or "That dolphin sleeps on a fluffy pillow!" or "That owl likes to watch TV!" Invite them to think of some silly sentences too.

ASK 'yes' and 'no' questions that will encourage them to think about how animals are cared for in a zoo. "Do you think the monkeys are cold at night?" "Do you think the tigers and lions like living in the zoo?" "Do you think the zoo keeper likes taking care of the animals?" "Do you think the animals like having people take pictures of them?" You can extend each question by saying, "How do you know?" or "What makes you think so?"

TEACH kids how to write a thank-you letter to the zoo by having them dictate what they would like to say while you write. You could do this using a dark marker on a paper plate. Then have kids draw a picture of what they saw at the zoo. Send it off to the zoo!

OLDER KIDS

SHOW kids a map of the zoo and let them plan out the agenda for the day. They can use a pen to mark which places they want to go to first, second, third, etc., and a route for how they will get there.

ASK them things like, "Why do you think zoos were invented?" "How would you change the zoo if you could?" "What would make the zoo nicer for all the animals?" "Which animal would you want to take home if you could?"

TEACH them how to play "I'm thinking of a zoo animal…" They can only ask you 'yes' and 'no' questions until they think they know which animal you are thinking of. Then let them have a turn while you ask them questions. A timeless brain game . . .

TRANSPORTATION

The many ways we travel from
place to place is truly wonderful.

TEACH WONDER...

For more information on how to
TEACH WONDER with your kids visit:
theteachableminute.com/teach

AIRPLANE

◇◇◇◇◇◇◇◇◇◇◇◇◇◇◇◇◇

Especially for Dads: *Kids like when we 'role play' with them. Consider turning your car into an airplane as you and your son or daughter sit in it while it's parked in the garage or driveway. You're the pilot and you've got a co-pilot with you. Maybe you can find some headphones for both of you as well. Now Captain, how will you play this out so they get a better understanding of what goes on in the cockpit of a plane?!*
Especially for Moms: *What do kids need to know about Amelia Earhart? Do they know what her role was in moving the aviation industry forward? Can they find an autobiography about her life? She is a hero for many kids. Teach heroes!*

YOUNGER KIDS

SHOW kids what a plane looks like and teach words that will extend their vocabulary. For instance, make a list of 'airplane words' and use these every time to show them a photo, video, or real airplane. Some important ones are wings, tail, engines, radar, cockpit, pilot, flight attendant, landing gear, seatbelt, and tray.

ASK questions that help them look for things on a picture of a plane or on a real plane. For instance, "Where is the window? You found one!" "Where are the wings? You found them!" "Where is the airplane's tail? You found it!" "Where does the pilot sit? You found the cockpit!" Continue like this, even if you have to give them clues or help the point. It keeps them physically and mentally engaged.

TEACH them how to buckle a seatbelt and turn on the overhead light. Kids learn these things VERY quickly when we let them practice.

OLDER KIDS

SHOW them a video of a plane taking off and landing (or take them to an airport to watch). How do they think a plane takes off and lands without crashing? Listen to their theories. Praise them for their thoughts. The idea is to lead them in a discussion and not to 'quiz' them. If they want to know more, find out together. Research is more fun when it's done collaboratively.

ASK them things like, "Why do you think people like to fly airplanes?" "Do you think it's hard?" "Why do you think that?" "Why do you we have to lift the window shades when the plane takes off and lands?" "Why does the pilot want us to wear our seatbelts even when the ride is not bumpy?" "What's an oxygen mask and why is there one for each person on a plane?"

TEACH kids how to do crossword puzzles and other 'thinking games.' Share some oldies, but goodies such as tic-tac-toe, connect the dots, and hangman. They can get back to their devices soon enough!

BICYCLE

◇◇◇◇◇◇◇◇◇◇◇◇◇◇◇◇◇

Especially for Grandparents: Tell kids what bicycles were like when you are a child. Maybe you could find a picture of one so you can show them how they are the same and different from the bikes we have today. Consider sharing the benefits of biking with kids…and the dangers. Kids remember what their Grandparents tell them!

YOUNGER KIDS

SHOW them things that start with a B like BICYCLE. Help them find pictures in magazines, coloring books, or old calendars of things that start with the 'b' sound. Show them how to arrange their 'b word' pictures into a collage on a manila folder. Write the word under each paper as they name it, emphasizing the sound of B like BICYCLE.

ASK kids what the names of the different parts are on a bike. "What's the name of the part that we use to steer the bike?" "What do we call the big round things on a bike?" "What's the name of the thing that warns people we that might hit them?" "What do we use to stop the bike?" If they don't know tell them…and keep asking them every now and then.

TEACH them by letting them practice. We can't ride a bike well without riding it in lots of places, lots of times.

OLDER KIDS

SHOW them how to look up bicycle in the dictionary or on Wikipedia and see if they can find other words that start with the prefix, 'bi.' Do they know what 'bi' means?

ASK questions that will help them decide on 5 things they want to know about bicycles. "Who invented the bicycle, and when?" "Why do you think bicycles have only two wheels and not several of them?" "How do think a bike stays 'up' when we're on it?" "How do bike brakes work?" "What does the most expensive bike in the world cost?"

TEACH them how to clean a bike. What do they need to know and how should they do it?

BOAT

◇◇◇◇◇◇◇◇◇◇◇

"Our middle son liked to figure things out on his own. When he was about 13 years old, we let him take his younger brother out in the row boat on the pond near where we lived. They both had life jackets on and they were going to go out to the middle of the pond to fish. They had done this many time with us so we felt they were ready to enjoy a brotherly adventure. After a little while my husband heard them shouting and he ran down to the woods to see what was up. It turns out the rope on the anchor disconnected from the row boat, one oar had fallen into the pond, and they had drifted down to the other end of the pond quickly when the wind picked up. The row boat was stuck in a patch of tall weeds and they couldn't move. It was too shallow to fish, so they figured they would start shouting. What were they shouting? "SOS, SOS, SOS!" Guess you might say we found the teachable minute when they got back!"

—Barbra, Chatham, MA

YOUNGER KIDS

SHOW kids how to sing the song, "Row, Row, Row Your Boat" and how to pretend that they are actually in a boat when they sing it. The bathtub is a great place to sing this timeless, catchy tune. Give them wooden spoons so they can row!

ASK them if can name all the different boats you point to on a chart or in the marina. Give them a few clues until they learn them. "Can you name this boat with the sails?" "Can you name this one with a periscope?" "Can you name this GIANT boat that carries a lot of people on it?" "Can you name this boat that needs paddles to make it go?" "Can you name this boat that takes people to islands?" If they don't know, tell them and keep asking them!

TEACH kids how to put on a life jacket all by themselves. Let them wear it in the bathtub, the pool, and the sprinkler. This way, they won't balk if they go on a boat and have to wear one.

OLDER KIDS

SHOW them how to find books about boats and boating in the library or on the internet. Once they find them, how will they choose the ones they want to read? **SHOW** them how to scan the Table of Contents and the Index or show them how they can read a description and some reviews of the book online.

ASK kids questions that help them understand how boats are the same and different from one another. "What do you think a yacht and a row boat have in common?" "How is a kayak different from a canoe?" "What are all the ways that a ferry boat is like a cruise ship?" Get them thinking about the concept of 'same and different.'

TEACH them about the importance of boats and help them make a list of all the ways that boats have helped the world become a better place.

BUS

Especially for Grandparents: Many kids are fearful of taking a bus even though many of them won't admit it. They have grown accustomed to being in a safe car with people they live with! Suddenly they find themselves on a bus with lots of kids and people. What can you tell them about protecting themselves, their belongings, and their sanity while riding a bus?!

YOUNGER KIDS

SHOW kids a large picture or a drawing of a bus. Label each part, using a bold dark marker, as they watch you write and say each thing. For example, wheel, door, window, windshield, headlight, bus number, top, bottom, back, front, etc. Then together, point to each part and read the label for it.

ASK questions that help them identify first and last sounds in 3-letter words. "What sound does BUS start with?" "What sound does CAT end with?" "What sound does FOX start with?" "What sound does POP start with and end with?" "What sound does RED end with?"

TEACH kids different ways of coping with 'bus situations' should they arise. For instance, discuss what they should do if they feel sick while on a bus. Tell them you would do if you forgot to get off at the right bus stop. Share your personal stories about things that happened on buses. If you don't have any, make them up! Kids learn much from stories.

Older Kids

SHOW kids what a bus station is like. Where is the ticket counter or kiosk for picking up a ticket? What do they need to look for on the bus schedule information board? Where do people wait for buses to arrive? How do you know you're on the right bus? Bus stations are cool places!

ASK questions that will lead to critical thinking. For example, "Why are buses shaped like they are?" "What are the differences between a city bus and a tour bus?" "Why is there a front and rear door on every bus?" "Which do you think is more fun? Riding a train or a bus? Why do you think so?" "Why were buses invented?"

TEACH them how to interpret a bus schedule, either online or in a brochure. Ask them to find different things on it. For instance, "What days of the week does a bus go from this city to this airport?" "What times do they leave?" Teach kids how to search for information.

CAR

◇◇◇◇◇◇◇◇◇

Especially for Dads: *What's under that mysterious hood, Dad? Kids want to know!*

Especially for Moms: *Kids are very attached to their cars. Consider letting them take pictures of the inside and outside of their car with a disposable camera. Even little ones can use one. Encourage them to take pictures of all different things such as the rear view mirror, the glove compartment, the steering wheel, the engine, and the license plate. They will think of plenty more things they want to 'shoot'...those are just a few to help them learn the names of car things.*

YOUNGER KIDS

SHOW them a car lot and take them on a tour so they can see all the different kinds and colors of cars there are.

ASK kids questions about cars so they learn can match the word with the object. "Where are the headlights?" "Can you say, 'headlights?'" "Here they are!" "Where are the windshield wipers?" "Can you say, 'windshield wipers?'" "Here they are!" "Where is the steering wheel?" "Can you say, 'steering wheel'? "Here it is!" "Where is your car seat?" "Can you say, car seat?" "Here it is!" Now get in it please!

TEACH kids lots of songs and tell them loads of stories when they are in the car and can't go anywhere! For little ones, sing lots of versions of "Baa Baa Black Sheep," changing 'baa baa' to 'mama' and 'papa' and 'lala.' For kids who are a little older, tell stories with a moral, for example, stories about stealing, lying, going with strangers, and smoking. They will listen attentively and ask you to tell those stories over and over again. SO true!

OLDER KIDS

SHOW them how to protect themselves if they are ever in the car alone and someone comes up to it. The best way is to teach them to press down on the horn without letting go until the stranger goes away. It works every time.

ASK questions that help them understand what a speedometer, odometer, fuel gauge, side-view mirror, rear-view mirror, washer fluid, and defroster is. "Why do you think we need a speedometer in every car that is made?" "Why would we need a side-view mirror if we have a rear-view mirror?" "How does a window defroster melt ice and snow?" They may want to look up some of these things. Even if they don't, keep asking questions like these, whenever you can.

TEACH them how to do crossword puzzles, Sudoku, and other games like these while they are in the car. Help them create a healthy balance between thinking games, video games, movies, books, and tech apps.

SUBWAY

◇◇◇◇◇◇◇◇◇◇◇◇◇◇◇◇

"My Father used to take the subway to work every morning and every night. He told us that one day he was on the subway, feeling weary and tired from working seven days a week. He said that he opened his eyes and saw some graffiti scribbled on the wall next to him. He read it out loud, slowly: "Never, Never, Never Give Up..." That was the 'teachable minute' that found him and helped him. And who was the teacher who said that? Winston Churchill."

—George, Ossining, NY

YOUNGER KIDS

SHOW kids what a subway looks like and point out things on it so they will learn more about it. If you can take them on a subway, take them! While you're on it, build their vocabulary by pointing to things and saying what they are such as, seat, railing, door, people, girl, boy, man, woman, backpack, map, sign, light, etc.

ASK them questions that help them think about this form of transportation. They may not know the answers, but we still want to ask them so we can encourage them to find out what they are! "What does a subway train look like? Let's find a book with pictures of one so we can see." "Why are subways only in the city? I wonder why?" "Why are subways do subways mostly travel under the ground? Let's find out."

TEACH them how to find books about subways in the library. Teach them how to ask the librarian for books. It is important that they know how to ask for help. They are not too young to learn that!

OLDER KIDS

SHOW kids a picture or video of a subway and ask them to tell you what they notice about it. See if they can find out why it was originally called a SUBWAY? Can they draw a picture of a subway? If you can take them on a real one, all the better! Take a pad and pencil so they can sketch one. Do they know what 'sketch' is?

ASK questions that help them learn 'pros and cons' or 'advantages and disadvantages' about taking the subway when we're in a major city. "Why do you think people would rather take the subway than a taxi cab?" "What does a taxi cab do that a subway can't do?" "Do you think the subway is better for people who live in the city or for people who are just visiting the city?" "Is a subway safer than a taxi cab during the day? What about at night?" See what they think!

TEACH kids how to protect a purse, wallet, cell phone, or backpack. What do they need to know? Even if they can't ride a subway, teach them anyway! It's important to know how to protect ourselves and our things, without being afraid.

TAXI CAB

◇◇◇◇◇◇◇◇◇◇◇◇◇◇◇◇◇◇◇

Especially for Dads: *Pretend you are a taxi cab driver and your kids are the passengers. Can you teach them what to say and do if they need to take a cab somewhere? Maybe you can even find a cap to play the role!*

Especially for Moms: *Do you have a phone book? Consider showing kids how to look up 'taxi cab' in the yellow pages. What information will they find? Have them practice looking up other things in the yellow pages. For example, ask them where should we look in the yellow pages if the toilet breaks down?!*

Younger Kids

SHOW them what a taxi cab looks like either on the street or in a toy store. What do they see? Wheels, windows, a cab driver, a trunk, doors, windshield wipers, a taxi sign on the roof, and headlights? What else do they notice? What color is it?

ASK them questions that will help build their imagination. For example, "Can you make a taxi cab out of a shoe box? What supplies will you need?" "Can you build a taxi cab out of play dough or clay?" "Can you paint a taxi cab on your easel? What colors will you need?"

TEACH kids how to say ask people how they are. Let them practice saying, "How are you today?" to people that they meet. Tell them that they will want to say, "Hi. How are you today?" when they get into a cab someday. That's what kind and nice people do!

OLDER KIDS

SHOW kids how to make a 'thinking web' by drawing a circle in the middle of a sheet of paper or on a whiteboard. Inside the circle, have them write 'taxi cab.' Coming off the circle, they should draw five lines that look like the rays of the sun. At the top of each ray, they should write a question that they want to investigate about taxi cabs! Thinking webs help kids learn and grow.

ASK kids to make predictions about the future of taxi cabs. "Do you think taxis will be around when you have children?" "What makes you think that?" "Do you think taxis will look different when you are 20 years old?" "How do you think they will look?" "If there are taxi cabs in the future, would you like to drive one?" "Why would someone like to be a cab driver?"

TEACH kids how to read the cab meter and add a tip for the driver. If the meter shows, $7.10, how much should they give the cab driver? If the meter shows, $15.95, how much should they pay? Do lots of those until they can figure out the tip in their heads.

TRAIN

◇◇◇◇◇◇◇◇◇◇◇◇◇

"I wish that all kids could learn the song "I've Been Working on the Railroad." Why? Because it is song that makes everybody feel good. If you don't know it, ask an elderly person to sing it for you. They know it…and so should kids! Music IS a 'teachable minute' because it is the universal language. How long has it been since you sang that song?!"
—Charlie, Roanoke, VA

YOUNGER KIDS

SHOW kids what a train station looks like. Most towns and cities have renovated their train stations. Take the kids on a 'field trip' to train station and enjoy all the marvelous things that you can show them while you are there. Kids are curious about trains.

ASK them questions after you read them "The Little Engine That Could" by Watty Piper. "Why do you think the little engine didn't want to go up the hill?" "Why were the toys feeling sad?" "Why did the little engine start to say, "I think I can, I think I can?" "What did you learn from this book?"

TEACH them how to count the train cars on a train when you draw different ones for them. Draw a train with only three cars attached and say, "How many train cars are there? Use your pointer finger and show me." Then write numbers on the cars, from left to right. Repeat this several times, with a different number of attached cars every time. Encourage kids to count them backwards too!

Older Kids

SHOW them a timeline of how trains have evolved since they were first invented. Timelines can be found in encyclopedias or on the internet. What do they need to know about understanding a timeline? What do timelines teach us? What did they learn about trains by studying the timeline of trains over time?

ASK kids questions that will lead to more questions. "What do you think would happen if one of the train cars came off the railroad track?" "What do you think the train conductor would do if a moose or a deer was on the track, right in front of the train while it was moving?" "What happens when people fall asleep or forget to get off at the right train stop?" "What are all the things a train would need to have on it if it was taking people from New York to California?"

TEACH appreciation and wonder. How in the world did train tracks come to be all over the world?

There is no end to where and when you can catch

the Teachable MINUTE

For details on how to receive
free downloadable materials, please visit:
www.theteachableminute.com

77 Books for 77 Places

◇◇◇

Around Town

DK Eyewitness Books: *Money* by Joe Cribb (Sep 5, 2005) Publisher: DK CHILDREN

Money Doesn't Grow On Trees: A Parent's Guide to Raising Financially Responsible Children by Neale S. Godfrey, Carolina Edwards and Tad Richards (Aug 1, 2006) Publisher: Touchstone

The Energy Bus for Kids: A Story about Staying Positive and Overcoming Challenges by Jon Gordon (Aug 21, 2012) Publisher: Wiley

Five Little Monkeys Wash the Car by Eileen Christelow (Aug 23, 2004) Publisher: Sandpiper; Reprint edition

The Little Bitty Bakery by Leslie Muir and Betsy Lewin (Aug 30, 2011) Publisher: Hyperion Book

Fast Food by Joost Elffers, Joost Elffers Saxton Freymann and Saxton Freymann (Mar 1, 2006) Publisher: Arthur A. Levine Books

Gas Station Charlie by Karen G. Kraushaar and Doris Kays Kraushaar (Dec 1, 1999) Publisher: Kays

Off We Go to the Grocery Store (Off We Go! series/U.S. edition) by Avril Webster and David Ryley (Feb 11, 2011) Publisher: Woodbine House; 1st American edition

Funky Junk: Cool Stuff to Make with Hardware (Kids Can Do It) by Renee Schwarz (Feb 1, 2003) Publisher: Kids Can Press

The Ice Cream Store by Dennis Lee and David McPhail (Sep 1992) Publisher: Scholastic Trade

Aunt Lily's Laundromat by Melanie Hope Greenberg (Sep 1, 1994) Publisher: Dutton Juvenile

Library Lion by Michelle Knudsen and Kevin Hawkes (Jun 25, 2009) Publisher: Candlewick

Only One Neighborhood by Marc Harshman and Barbara Garrison (Sep 6, 2007) Publisher: Dutton Juvenile

My Dad Is the Best Playground by Luciana Navarro Powell (May 8, 2012) Publisher: Robin Corey Books; Brdbk edition

The Jolly Postman by Allan Ahlberg and Janet Ahlberg (Sep 1, 2001) Publisher: LB Kids

David Goes To School by David Shannon (Aug 1, 1999) Publisher: Blue Sky Press

HOME

A Chair for My Mother 25th Anniversary Edition (Reading Rainbow Books) by Vera B. William (Aug 1, 1984) Publisher: Greenwillow Books; Rei Rep edition

Dinosaurs in My Basement by Deborah Lomax-Reid (Feb 21, 2012) Publisher: Xlibris Corporation

There's a Boy in the Girls' Bathroom by Louis Sachar (Aug 12, 1988) Publisher: Yearling; Reprint edition

Uncle John's Did You Know?: Bathroom Reader for Kids Only (Uncle John's Bathroom Reader for Kids Only) by Bathroom Readers' Institute (Nov 9, 2006) Publisher: Portable Press

Kid Talk: Conversation Cards for the Entire Family (Tabletalk Conversation Cards) by U S. Games Systems Inc. (Aug 2002) Publisher: United States Games Systems

The Millionaire Kids Club — Garage Sale Riches by Lynnette Khalfani-Cox Susan Beacham (Feb 5, 2008) Publisher: Advantage World Press; 1st edition

In the Night Kitchen (Caldecott Collection) by Maurice Sendak (Jan 18, 1996) Publisher: HarperCollins

Tell Me A Story Mama by Angela Johnson and David Soman (Sep 1, 1992) Publisher: Scholastic

Ultimate Guide: Porches (Home Improvement) by Steve Cory, Home Improvement, Porches and How-To (Jun 6, 2011) Publisher: Creative Homeowner

Crumbs on the Stairs — Migas en las escaleras: A Mystery in English & Spanish by Karl Beckstrand (Jun 1, 2011) Publisher: Premio Publishing & Gozo Books, LLC

Little Critter: The Best Yard Sale by Mercer Mayer (Jul 27, 2010) Publisher: HarperFestival

PUBLIC PLACES

Richard Scarry's A Day at the Airport (Pictureback(R)) by Richard Scarry (Apr 24, 2001) Publisher: Random House Books for Young Readers

Apartment Book by Leo Hartas and Richard Platt (Sep 9, 1995) Publisher: DK CHILDREN

The Bookstore Ghost (Penguin Young Readers, L2) by Barbara Maitland and Nadine Bernard Westcott (Sep 1, 1998) Publisher: Penguin Young Readers

Over My Dead Body (43 Old Cemetery Road) by Kate Klise and M. Sarah Klise (Sep 6, 2011) Publisher: Sandpiper; Reprint edition

Disney Mickey Mouse Clubhouse Movie Theater: Storybook and Movie Projector by Tisha Hamilton, Disney Mickey Mouse

Clubhouse and Disney Storybook Artists (Aug 7, 2012) Publisher: Reader's Digest; Har/Toy edition

Dare To Dream!: 25 Extraordinary Lives by Sandra McLeod Humphrey (Mar 11, 2005) Publisher: Prometheus Books

Fancy Nancy and the Fabulous Fashion Boutique by Jane O'Connor and Robin Preiss Glasser (Oct 12, 2010) Publisher: HarperCollins

Portion Size Me: A Kid-Driven Plan to a Healthier Family by Alexandra Reid and Marshall Reid (Apr 1, 2012) Publisher: Sourcebooks

Brush Your Teeth Please Pop-Up by Leslie Mcguire and Jean Pidgeon (Apr 1, 1993) Publisher: Reader's Digest; Pop edition

The Ghost at the Drive-In Movie (The Boxcar Children Mysteries #116) by Gertrude Chandler Warner (Jan 1, 2008) Publisher: Albert Whitman & Company

Alligator In The Elevator by Rick Charette (Jun 1, 1998) Publisher: Pine Point Record Co.

Elevator/escalator Book by Bob Barner (Aug 1, 1990) Publisher: Doubleday Books for Young Readers

The Eye Book (Bright & Early Books(R)) by Theo. LeSieg and Joe Mathieu (Sep 28, 1999) Publisher: Random House Books for Young Readers; First Edition

The Fire Station (Classic Munsch) by Robert N. Munsch and Michael Martchenko (Feb 1, 1992) Publisher: Annick Press

At the Flower Shop: Learning Simple Division by Forming Equal Groups by Jennifer Nowark (May 30, 2003) Publisher: Rosen Publishing Group

Animal Crackers: A Tender Book About Death and Funerals and Love by Bridget Marshall and Ron Boldt (Oct 1, 1998) Publisher: Centering Corp

Going to the Hospital (First Experiences) by Fred Rogers (Sep 22, 1997) Publisher: Puffin

The Hotel Cat (New York Review Children's Collection) by Esther Holden Averill (Sep 30, 2005) Publisher: NYR Children's Collection

The Mystery in the Mall (The Boxcar Children Mysteries #72) by Gertrude Chandler Warner (Sep 1, 1999) Publisher: Albert Whitman & Company

Ben: The Very Best Furry Friend —, A children's book about a therapy dog and the friends he makes at the library and nursing home by Holly Raus and Preston George Pysh (Feb 16, 2011) Publisher: Pylon Publishing

My Friend the Doctor by Joanna Cole and Maxie Chambliss (Jul 26, 2005) Publisher: HarperFestival

The Pet Shop Revolution by Ana Juan (Oct 1, 2011) Publisher: Arthur A. Levine Books

The Police Station (Our Community) by David Armentrout and Patricia Armentrout (Sep 9, 2011) Publisher: Rourke Publishing

Squirrel World: A Park Pals Adventure (Park Pals Adventures) by Johanna Hurwitz and Kathi McCord (Aug 23, 2007) Publisher: Chronicle Books; First Edition

Gorilla Garage by Mark Shulman and Vincent Nguyen (Mar 1, 2009) Publisher: Amazon Children's Publishing

Who's in the Bathroom? by Jeanne Willis and Adrian Reynolds (Mar 27, 2007) Publisher: Simon & Schuster Children's Publishing

National Geographic Kids Ultimate U.S. Road Trip Atlas: Maps, Games, Activities, and More for Hours of Backseat Fun by Crispin Boyer (Mar 13, 2012) Publisher: National Geographic Children's Books

Froggy Eats Out by Jonathan London and Frank Remkiewicz (Jun 23, 2003) Publisher: Puffin

Those Shoes by Maribeth Boelts and Noah Z. Jones (Jun 9, 2009) Publisher: Candlewick; Reprint edition

Where the Sidewalk Ends 30th Anniversary Edition: Poems and Drawings by Shel Silverstein (Jan 20, 2004) Publisher: HarperCollins; 30 Anv edition

I Want to Be a Veterinarian by Catherine O'Neill Grace (Mar 15, 1999) Publisher: Sandpiper

PUBLIC PLACES

Tickets to Ride: An Alphabetic Amusement by Mark Rogalski (Oct 10, 2006) Publisher: Running Press Kids

The Everything Kids' Baseball Book: From baseball history to player stats — with lots of homerun fun in between! (Everything Kids Series) by Greg Jacobs (Mar 18, 2010) Publisher: Adams Media; 6th edition

Basketball: How It Works (The Science of Sports) by Suzanne Slade (Apr 1, 2010) Publisher: Capstone Press

Clam-I-Am!: All About the Beach (Cat in the Hat's Learning Library) by Tish Rabe and Aristides Ruiz (May 24, 2005) Publisher: Random House Books for Young Readers

Bowling in Action (Sports in Action) by Niki Walker, Sarah Dann and Marc Crabtree (Mar 15, 2003) Publisher: Crabtree Publishing Company

Toasting Marshmallows: Camping Poems by Kristine O'Connell George and Kate Kiesler (Apr 2001) Publisher: Clarion Books

Sports Illustrated Kids Football Playbook: Games, Activities, Puzzles and Fun! by Sports Illustrated Kids (Nov 8, 2011) Publisher: Sports Illustrated; Original edition

Build Your Own Mini Golf Course, Lemonade Stand, and Other Things to Do (Build It Yourself) by Tammy Enz (Jan 2, 2011) Publisher: Capstone Press

Museum Trip by Barbara Lehman (May 22, 2006) Publisher: Houghton Mifflin Books for Children

101 Cool Pool Games for Children: Fun and Fitness for Swimmers of All Levels (SmartFun Activity Books) by Kim Rodomista and Robin Patterson (Aug 18, 2006) Publisher: Hunter House

The View at the Zoo by Kathleen Long Bostrom and Guy Francis (Apr 1, 2011) Publisher: Ideals Children's Books, Ideals Publications

TRANSPORTATION

Airplanes: Soaring! Diving! Turning! by Patricia Hubbell, Megan Halsey and Sean Addy (Oct 2011) Publisher: Amazon Children's Publishing

Wheels of Change: How Women Rode the Bicycle to Freedom (With a Few Flat Tires Along the Way) by Sue Macy (Jan 11, 2011) Publisher: National Geographic Children's Books

How to Draw Planes, Trains and Boats (Dover How to Draw) by Barbara Soloff-Levy (Nov 24, 2008) Publisher: Dover Publications

The Little School Bus by Carol Roth and Pamela Paparone (Jun 1, 2004) Publisher: North-South Books

If I Built a Car by Chris Van Dusen (Jun 14, 2007) Publisher: Puffin; Reprint edition

New York City Subway Trains: 12 Classic Punch and Build Trains by New York Transit Museum (Nov 25, 2003) Publisher: Gibbs Smith

The Adventures of Taxi Dog (Picture Puffins) by Debra Barracca, Sal Barracca and Mark Buehner (Mar 1, 2000) Publisher: Puffin

Big Book Of Trains by DK Publishing (Oct 12, 1998) Publisher: DK CHILDREN

Teachable Minute Lines

- I love you
- Great idea
- Way to go
- You are wonderful
- I am amazed
- That's a great way to think about that
- Fantastic job
- What a good listen
- I trust you
- You figured it out
- I like the way you wrote that
- That's what good readers do
- You are so special
- What a smart answer
- Hurray for you
- Beautiful work
- You are thinking
- I feel so proud of you
- You are amazing me
- Such incredible thinking
- Super job
- You really worked hard
- I like the way you explained that
- You mean so much to me
- What a ton of work
- How amazing are you?

- Remarkable
- You have such a wonderful imagination
- Is there anything you can't fix?
- You always make me laugh
- What do you think?
- I never thought of that
- You are SO smart
- Look at how many things you know
- That is so well done
- You figured that out by yourself
- I did not know that
- What makes you think that?
- You are so much fun to be with
- Great sense of humor
- I like the choice you made
- You are so positive
- I knew you could come up with something
- What would you say?
- That takes a lot of work
- Incredible performance
- You really care
- I respect your thinking on that
- You didn't give up
- What a fun kid you are
- Such a good listener
- This is so well done
- How amazing is that?
- What would you do?
- Can you help me?
- Your ideas are fantastic
- Beautiful job

- I never knew that
- You always find a way
- What a great discovery
- Wow
- You are such a good friend
- I like the way you wonder about things
- Unbelievable
- Why do you think so?
- What's another way?
- How do you know?
- You learned so much
- Look at how far you've come
- I like you
- You are such a good friend
- That is such a smart thing to say
- You amaze me
- How funny is that?
- You gave that so much thought
- I love you, no matter what

Note from Dr. Connie...

Dear Reader,

I truly want you to reap the rewards that come with being your child's first and most important teacher on the planet, as I have!

I can promise you that your kids will grow smarter and more appreciative if you make time to catch the teachable minute often. Use the power of teaching. It's powerful.

And remember...

Keep your eye on the child and not on the modern devices that we have all become dependent on so you can enjoy millions of teachable minutes with your kids and with their kids! Go catch them all . . .

With loving support,
Connie Hebert

One more thing...

For details on how to receive free downloadable materials, please visit: www.theteachableminute.com

CPSIA information can be obtained at www.ICGtesting.com
Printed in the USA
BVOW07s1650270813

329558BV00001B/10/P